FINDING OUR LOST HAPPINESS

Books by His Divine Grace
A. C. Bhaktivedanta Swami Prabhupāda:

Bhagavad-gītā As It Is
Śrīmad-Bhāgavatam (1st to 12th Cantos)
Śrī Caitanya-Caritāmṛta (9 vols.)
Kṛṣṇa, The Supreme Personality of Godhead
Teachings of Lord Caitanya
The Nectar of Devotion
The Nectar of Instruction
Śrī Īśopaniṣad
Light of the Bhāgavata
Easy Journey to Other Planets
The Science of Self-Realization
Kṛṣṇa Consciousness: The Topmost Yoga System
Perfect Questions, Perfect Answers
Teachings of Lord Kapila, the Son of Devahuti
Transcendental Teachings of Prahlāda Mahārāja
Teachings of Queen Kuntī
Kṛṣṇa, the Reservoir of Pleasure
The Path of Perfection
Life Comes from Life
Message of Godhead
The Perfection of Yoga
Beyond Birth and Death
On the Way to Kṛṣṇa
Rāja-vidyā: The King of Knowledge
Elevation to Kṛṣṇa Consciousness
Kṛṣṇa Consciousness: The Matchless Gift
Selected Verses from the Vedic Scriptures
Back to Godhead magazine (founder)

A complete catalogue is available upon request.
The Bhaktivedanta Book Trust, ISKCON Temple,
Hare Krishna Land, Juhu, Mumbai 400 049. India.
The above books are also available at ISKCON centers.
Please contact a center near to your place.

FINDING OUR LOST HAPPINESS

His Divine Grace

A.C. Bhaktivedanta Swami Prabhupāda

Founder-*Ācārya* of the International Society for Krishna Consciousness

The Bhaktivedanta Book Trust

Cover Design: The cover image depicts the transformation of the heart from a barren desert-like state of disappointment to the lush green state of fulfillment

---

Readers interested in the subject matter of this book are invited by The Bhaktivedanta Book Trust to correspond with its secretary at the following address:

The Bhaktivedanta Book Trust
Hare Krishna Land
Juhu, Mumbai 400 049, India

Website / E-mail :
www.indiabbt.com
admin@indiabbt.com

Finding Our Lost Happiness (English)

1st printing, April 2013: 20,000 copies

ISBN: 978-93-82716-66-2

Published and Printed by
The Bhaktivedanta Book Trust

HRG4

CONTENTS

Introduction

The Vedic literature has prophesised about this present age of quarrel and hypocrisy or the *Kali-yuga*. The *Kali-yuga* means the fourth age. There are four different kinds of ages in the vedic time-line: *Satya-yuga*, *Tretā-yuga*, *Dvāpara-yuga*, and *Kali-yuga*. Just like there are six seasons, or four seasons in a year, similarly, in one day of *Brahmā* there are one hundred cycles of four *yugas*. Four *yugas* means forty-three hundred thousands of years. It is a very long period. That is the duration of four *yugas*. When one thousand *yugas* pass, then one day of *Brahmā*—twelve hours are finished. It is a big calculation. Anyway, there are four *yugas*—*Satya-yuga*, *Dvāpara-yuga*, *Tretā-yuga*, and *Kali-yuga*.

In *Satya-yuga*, the religious principles are followed strictly, cent percent. That is called *Satya-yuga*. And in *Tretā-yuga*, twenty-five percent reduced. That means seventy-five percent religious principles and twenty-five percent irreligious. And in the *Dvāpara-yuga*, fifty-fifty: fifty percent religious and fifty percent irreligious. And the *Kali-yuga*, seventy-five percent irreligious and twenty-five percent religious, gradually reducing to nil—no more religion. Then finished. Then there will be devastation. Again *Satya-yuga* will begin. This is the way of change of *Satya-yuga-Satya*, *Tretā*, *Dvāpara*, *Kali*. The duration of *Satya-yuga* is about eighteen hundred thousand of years. Eighteen hundred thousands of years. Similarly, *Tretā-yuga*, about twelve hundred thousands of years. Similarly,

Dvāpara-yuga, eight hundred thousands of years. And *Kali-yuga* four hundred thousands of years. This is the beginning of *Kali-yuga*. Out of about four hundred thousands of years, we have passed only 5,000 years. *Kali-yuga* has begun just after the Battle of Kurukṣetra. So we have passed only about 5,000 years of this *Kali-yuga* and 4,27,000 years are still in balance.

The *Śrīmad-Bhāgavatam*, which was written five thousand years ago by Veda Vyāsa , an incarnation of the Lord Himself, predicted the symptoms of the current age of quarrel and hypocrisy or *Kali-Yuga*. A few of these symptoms are described as:

"With the progress of this age, *Kali-yuga*, *dharma*, religious principles; *satyam*, truthfulness; śaucam, cleanliness; *kṣamā*, forgiveness; *dayā*, mercifulness; *āyuḥ*, duration of life; *balam*, bodily strength and *smṛtiḥ*, memory will gradually reduce to nil, almost nil."

"*vittam eva kalau nṝṇām*. If you get money somehow or other, then everything is there. You may be a third-class, fourth-class, tenth-class man, but if you get money some way or other, then you are very respectable. There is no question of your culture or aristocracy or education or knowledge. This is *Kali-yuga*."

"*dharma-nyāya-vyavasthāyāṁ kāraṇaṁ balam eva hi*. And if you have got some influence, strength, then in your favor everything will be decided. You are the most irreligious person, but if you can bribe the priestly order, he will certify, 'Yes, you are religious.' So money, not actual qualification."

"*avṛttyā nyāya-daurbalyaṁ pāṇḍitye cāpalaṁ vacaḥ*. If you have no money, then you will never get justice in the court. If a man talks expertly, it doesn't matter what he talks. Even if nobody understands him, he is *paṇḍita* or scholar."

"*anāḍhyataivāsādhutve sādhutve dambha eva tu, svīkāra eva codvāhe snānam eva prasādhanam* . *Anāḍhyatā*. If you are poor man, then you are dishonest. People will understand that 'This man is actually not honest because he does not know how to earn money by hook or crook.'"

"*satyatve dhārṣṭyam eva hi.* And one who will simply play jugglery of words, he will be considered as very truthful."

"*dākṣyaṁ kuṭumba-bharaṇam.* One shall be considered very expert if he can maintain his family—wife and children. That means this will be difficult. It has already become difficult. To maintain wife and a few children, that is also a great burden at the present moment. Therefore nobody wants to marry."

Human society, at the present moment, is not in the darkness of oblivion. It has made rapid progress in the field of material comforts, education and economic development throughout the entire world. But there is a pinprick somewhere in the social body at large, and therefore there are large-scale quarrels, even over less important issues. There is need of a clue as to how humanity can become one in peace, friendship and prosperity with a common cause.

The gross materialists, who cannot see beyond materialistic activities, find it impossible to believe that besides our material universe, a spiritual universe exists. Completely identifying with the body, such materialists are like animals, simply eating, sleeping, mating, and defending. They are so captivated by these four animalistic propensities that they lose the power to discriminate between sinful and pious activities. They tirelessly endeavor for a little sense gratification, but all their efforts end in futility. Many modern scientists have taken up the role of priests facilitating such gross activities, which are unbeneficial and fatal. These scientists have made available a variety of products meant simply to titillate the senses, thus creating a deadly competitive mood among the materialists, which has in turn caused an obnoxious atmosphere in society. People think they become free and independent through such sensual activities, but factually they become more tightly bound up in chains. The greater their accumulated wealth, the greater their anxiety and depravity. As much as they try to usurp the Supreme Lord's position of being the only enjoyer, that much and more are they drawn into the jaws of a horrible death. And these activities make a Herculean task out of such a simple and basic activity as sustaining the body, which needs a little nourishment only.

The endeavors human beings have made to establish a close and harmonious relationship with one another have culminated in the United Nations. This organization is based on the concept of the family unit. The gradual expansion of the family unit to a large community, to a village, to a state, to a country, and finally to a continent has given the clue for the formation of the United Nations. The thing to be noted, however, is its center. What is the central attraction? If the process of expansion were reversed, we would end up with the human body as the basic unit. The senses are of prime importance in the body; more important than the senses is the mind, then intelligence, and finally the false ego. And more important than the false ego is the real self, a pure spiritual being that is part and parcel of the Supreme Lord, Viṣṇu. Therefore the conclusion is that the fountainhead of everything is Lord Viṣṇu. For this reason Prahlāda Mahārāja said,

"Persons who are strongly entrapped by the consciousness of enjoying material life, and who have therefore accepted as their leader or guru a similar blind man attached to external sense objects, cannot understand that the goal of life is to return home, back to Godhead, and engage in the service of Lord Viṣṇu."

Those who lose sight of the center and become attracted to the externals are shallow and misguided. These misguided persons are in a sense blind; hence the world cannot expect them to give any guidance toward enlightenment. However much these blind people may pretend to guide and benefit other blind people, factually they are fully controlled by the will of providence. We should make the effort to understand that the cause and source of everything is Lord Viṣṇu, the Absolute Truth, and that the fullest manifestation of this Absolute Truth is Lord Kṛṣṇa, the source of even Lord Viṣṇu. As Lord Kṛṣṇa says in the *Bhagavad-gītā* (7.7), "O conqueror of wealth, [Arjuna], there is no truth superior to Me."

Forgetfulness of the Supreme Lord, Viṣṇu, is human society's real and original disease. So, if one does not treat this ailment but instead shows insincere and shallow concern for the patients, one might give them some momentary relief and pleasure, but ultimately such a course of action cannot cure them permanently. If the patient goes for proper medicine and diet but is instead administered bad medicine and diet, then he is certainly in the jaws of death.

Disparity in human society is due to lack of principles in a godless civilization. There is God, or the Almighty One, from whom everything emanates, by whom everything is maintained and in whom everything is merged to rest. Material science has tried to find the ultimate source of creation very insufficiently, but it is a fact that there is one ultimate source of everything that be. This ultimate source is explained rationally and authoritatively in the beautiful *Bhāgavatam*, or *Śrīmad-Bhāgavatam*. After considerable deliberation, the sages in the past concluded that Lord Kṛṣṇa is the Supreme Being, the origin of all expansions and manifestations of the Supreme Absolute Truth. As the *Śrīmad-Bhāgavatam* (1.3.28) declares, "All of the abovementioned incarnations are either plenary portions or portions of the plenary portions of the Lord, but Lord Śrī Kṛṣṇa is the original Personality of Godhead..." The *Brahma-saṁhitā* (5.1) confirms this: "Kṛṣṇa who is known as Govinda is the Supreme Godhead. He has an eternal blissful spiritual body. He is the origin of all. He has no other origin and He is the prime cause of all causes."

Thus if we can transcend the material body and its physical relationships and become connected with everyone through the Lord Kṛṣṇa, the original Godhead, we can relate on a platform of truth and reality. Then the actual meaning of fraternity and equality will crystalize.

In this age of Kali, the Supreme Personality of Godhead appeared as Sri Caitanya Mahāprabhu and preached that in this age, the Vedic activities cannot be systematically performed because people are so fallen. He gave this recommendation from the śāstras:

harer nāma harer nāma
harer nāmaiva kevalam
kalau nāsty eva nāsty eva
nāsty eva gatir anyathā

(Bṛhan-nāradīya Purāṇa 3.8.126)

'In this Age of Kali there is no other means, no other means, no other means for self-realization than chanting the holy name, chanting the holy name, chanting the holy name of Lord Hari.'

The Kṛṣṇa consciousness movement is therefore teaching people all over the world how to chant the *Hare Kṛṣṇa* mantra, and this has proved very much effective in all places at all times. The Supreme Personality of Godhead appears in order to teach us Vedic principles intended for understanding Him (*vedais ca sarvair aham eva vedyah*). One should not mistake the body of Kṛṣṇa or Caitanya Mahāprabhu to be a material body like ours, for Kṛṣṇa and Caitanya Mahāprabhu appeared as needed for the benefit of the entire human society. Out of causeless mercy, the Lord appears in different ages in His original *śuddha-sattva* (transcendental) body to elevate human society to the spiritual platform upon which they can truly benefit. Unfortunately, modern politicians and other leaders stress the bodily comforts of life (*yasy-atma-buddhih kunape tri-dhatuke*) and concentrate on the activities of this *ism* and that *ism*, which they describe in different kinds of flowery language. Essentially such activities are the activities of animals (*sa eva go-kharah*). We should learn how to act from *Bhagavad-gītā*, which explains everything for human understanding. Thus we can become happy even in this age of Kali.

A student is to be considered perfected when he understands the identity of the holy name and the Supreme Lord. Unless one is under the shelter of a realized spiritual master, his understanding of the Supreme is simply foolishness. However, one can fully understand the transcendental Lord by service and devotion. Lord Caitanya declared that the Hare Kṛṣṇa mantra could at once deliver a conditioned soul from material contamination. In this age of Kali there is no alternative to chanting this *mahā-mantra*. It is stated that the essence of all Vedic literature is the chanting of this holy name of Kṛṣṇa:

Hare Kṛṣṇa, Hare Kṛṣṇa, Kṛṣṇa Kṛṣṇa, Hare Hare
Hare Rāma, Hare Rāma, Rāma Rāma, Hare Hare

In three out of the four millenniums (namely *Satya-yuga*, *Treta-yuga* and *Dvapara-yuga*) people had the honor to be able to understand transcendence through the path of disciplic succession. However, in the present age, people have no interest in the disciplic succession. Instead, they have invented many paths of logic and argument. This individual attempt to understand the supreme transcendence (called the ascending process) is not approved by the *Vedas*. The Absolute Truth must descend from the absolute platform. He is not to be understood by the ascending process.

The holy name of the Lord—Hare Kṛṣṇa, Hare Kṛṣṇa, Kṛṣṇa Kṛṣṇa, Hare Hare. Hare Rāma, Hare Rāma, Rāma Rāma, Hare Hare—is a transcendental vibration because it comes from the transcendental platform, the supreme abode of Kṛṣṇa. Because there is no difference between Kṛṣṇa and His name, the holy name of Kṛṣṇa is as pure, perfect and liberated as Kṛṣṇa Himself. Academic scholars have no entrance by means of logic and other argument into the understanding of the transcendental nature of the holy name of God. The single path in understanding the transcendental nature of 'Hare Kṛṣṇa, Hare Kṛṣṇa, Kṛṣṇa Kṛṣṇa, Hare Hare. Hare Rāma, Hare Rāma, Rāma Rāma, Hare Hare' is the chanting of these names with faith and adherence. Such chanting will release one from designated conditions arising from the gross and subtle bodies.

In this age of logic, argument and disagreement, the chanting of Hare Kṛṣṇa is the only means for self-realization. Because this transcendental vibration alone can deliver the conditioned soul, it is considered to be the essence of the *Vedānta-sūtra*. According to the material conception, there is duality between the name, form, quality, emotions and activities of a person and the person himself, but as far as the transcendental vibration is concerned, there is no such limitation, for it descends from the spiritual world. In the spiritual world there is no difference between the name of the person and the quality of the person.

"All Vedic rituals, mantras and understanding are compressed into eight words: Hare Kṛṣṇa, Hare Kṛṣṇa, Kṛṣṇa Kṛṣṇa, Hare Hare." Similarly, in the *Kali santaraṇa Upaniṣad* it is stated:

hare kṛṣṇa hare kṛṣṇa
kṛṣṇa kṛṣṇa hare hare

hare rāma hare rāma
rāma rāma hare hare
iti ṣoḍaśakaṁ nāmnāṁ
kali-kalmaṣa-nāśanaṁ
nātaḥ parataropāyaḥ
sarva-vedeṣu dṛśyate

(Kali-santaraṇa Upaniṣad)

"Hare Kṛṣṇa, Hare Kṛṣṇa, Kṛṣṇa Kṛṣṇa, Hare Hare/ Hare Rāma, Hare Rāma, Rāma Rāma, Hare Hare—these sixteen names composed of thirty-two syllables are the only means to counteract the evil effects of Kali-yuga.After searching through all the Vedic literature, one cannot find a method of religion more sublime for this age than the chanting of Hare Kṛṣṇa."

Section I

Ancient Prophecies Fulfilled

A little-known fact is that a book written over five thousand years ago—*Śrīmad-Bhāgavatam*—predicted many current trends and events with amazing accuracy. This description of the Kali-yuga [the present age of quarrel and hypocrisy] is given in the Twelfth Canto of *Śrīmad-Bhāgavatam. Śrīmad-Bhāgavatam* was written five thousand years ago, when the Kali-yuga was about to begin, and many things that would happen in the future are spoken of there. Therefore we accept *Śrīmad-Bhāgavatam* as *śāstra* [revealed scripture]. The compiler of *śāstra* (the *śāstra-kāra*) must be a liberated person so that he can describe past, present, and future.

In *Śrīmad-Bhāgavatam* you will find many things which are foretold. There is mention of Lord Buddha's appearance and Lord Kalki's appearance. (Lord Kalki will appear at the end of the Kali-yuga.) There is also mention of Lord Caitanya's appearance. Although the *Bhāgavatam* was written five thousand years ago, the writer knew past, present, and future (*tri-kāla-jña*), and thus he could predict all these events with perfect accuracy.

Śukadeva Gosvāmī, the speaker of *Śrīmad-Bhāgavatam* while describing the chief symptoms of this age says, *tataś cānudinam*: With the progress of this age [Kali-yuga], *dharma*, religious principles; *satyam*, truthfulness; *śaucam*, cleanliness; *kṣamā*, forgiveness; *dayā*, mercifulness; *āyuḥ*, duration of life; *balam*, bodily strength; *smṛti*, memory—these eight things will gradually decrease to nil or almost nil.

About present day society, the *Śrīmad-Bhāgavatam* prophesies:

prāyeṇālpāyuṣaḥ sabhya
kalāv asmin yuge janāḥ

mandāḥ sumanda-matayo
manda-bhāgyā hy upadrutāḥ

(Śrīmad-Bhāgavatam 1.1.10)

TRANSLATION

O learned one, in this iron age of Kali men have but short lives. They are quarrelsome, lazy, misguided, unlucky and, above all, always disturbed.

PURPORT

The devotees of the Lord are always anxious for the spiritual improvement of the general public. When the sages of Naimiṣāraṇya analyzed the state of affairs of the people in this age of Kali, they foresaw that men would live short lives. In Kali-yuga, the duration of life is shortened not so much because of insufficient food but because of irregular habits. By keeping regular habits and eating simple food, any man can maintain his health. Overeating, over-sense gratification, overdependence on another's mercy, and artificial standards of living sap the very vitality of human energy. Therefore the duration of life is shortened.

The people of this age are also very lazy, not only materially but in the matter of self-realization. The human life is especially meant for self-realization. That is to say, man should come to know what he is, what the world is, and what the supreme truth is. Human life is a means by which the living entity can end all the miseries of the hard struggle for life in material existence and by which he can return to Godhead, his eternal home. But, due to a bad system of education, men have no desire for self-realization. Even if they come to know about it, they unfortunately become victims of misguided teachers.

In this age, men are victims not only of different political creeds and parties, but also of many different types of sense-gratificatory diversions, such as cinemas, sports, gambling, clubs, mundane libraries, bad association, smoking, drinking, cheating, pilfering, bickerings, and so on. Their minds are always disturbed and full of anxieties due to so many different engagements. In this age, many unscrupulous men manufacture their own religious faiths which are not based on any revealed scriptures, and very often people who are addicted to sense gratification are attracted by such institutions. Consequently, in the name of religion so many sinful acts are being carried on that the people in general have neither peace of mind nor health of body. The student (*brahmacārī*) communities are no longer being maintained, and householders do not observe the rules and regulations of the *gṛhastha-āśrama*. Consequently, the so-called *vānaprasthas* and *sannyāsīs* who come out of such *gṛhastha-āśramas* are easily deviated from the rigid path. In the Kali-yuga the whole atmosphere is surcharged with faithlessness. Men are no longer interested in spiritual values. Material sense gratification is now the standard of civilization. For the maintenance of such material civilizations, man has formed complex nations and communities, and there is a constant strain of hot and cold wars between these different groups. It has become very difficult, therefore, to raise the spiritual standard due to the present distorted values of human society. The sages of Naimiṣāraṇya are anxious to disentangle all fallen souls, and here they are seeking the remedy from Śrīla Sūta Gosvāmī.

So, *kaler doṣa-nidhe rājan*: The faults of this age are just like an ocean. If you were put into the Pacific Ocean, you would not know how to save your life. Even if you were a very expert swimmer, it would not be possible for you to cross the Pacific Ocean. Similarly, the Kali-yuga is described in the *Bhāgavatam* as an ocean of faults. It is infected with so many anomalies that there seems to be no way out. But there is one medicine: *kīrtanād eva kṛṣṇasya mukta-saṅgaḥ paraṁ vrajet* (*Śrīmad-Bhāgavatam* 12.3.51). Just like if there is some epidemic, disease, and if you take vaccine, it is supposed that you are free from the contamination. So this vaccine of chanting Hare Kṛṣṇa *mahā-mantra*— Hare Kṛṣṇa Hare Kṛṣṇa, Kṛṣṇa Kṛṣṇa, Hare Hare / Hare Rāma, Hare Rāma, Rāma Rāma, Hare Hare—will keep you fit without any contamination of this age of Kali.

CHAPTER 1

Śrīmad-Bhāgavatam, Canto Twelve, Chapter Two

"The Symptoms of Kali-yuga"

This chapter relates that, when the bad qualities of the age of Kali will increase to an intolerable level, the Supreme Personality of Godhead will descend as Kalki to destroy those who are fixed in irreligion. After that, a new *Satya-yuga* will begin.

As the age of Kali progresses, all good qualities of men diminish and all impure qualities increase. Atheistic systems of so-called religion become predominant, replacing the codes of Vedic law. The kings become just like highway bandits, the people in general become dedicated to low occupations, and all the social classes become just like *śūdras.* All cows become like goats, all spiritual hermitages become like materialistic homes, and family ties extend no further than the immediate relationship of marriage.

When the age of Kali has almost ended, the Supreme Personality of Godhead will incarnate. He will appear in the village Śambhala, in the home of the exalted *brāhmaṇa* Viṣṇuyaśā, and will take the name Kalki. He will mount His horse Devadatta and, taking His sword in hand, will roam about the earth killing millions of bandits in the guise of kings. Then the signs of the next Satya-yuga will begin to appear. When the moon, sun and the planet Bṛhaspati enter simultaneously into one constellation and conjoin in the lunar mansion Puṣyā, Satya-yuga will begin. In the order of Satya, Tretā, Dvāpara and Kali, the cycle of four ages rotates in the society of living entities in this universe.

The chapter ends with a brief description of the future dynasties of the sun and moon coming from Vaivasvata Manu in the next Satya-yuga. Even now two saintly *kṣatriyas* are living who at the end of this Kali-yuga will reinitiate the pious dynasties of the sun god, Vivasvān, and the moon god, Candra. One of these kings is Devāpi, a brother of Mahārāja Śantanu, and the other is Maru, a descendant of Ikṣvāku. They are biding their time incognito in a village named Kalāpa.

TEXT 1

śrī-śuka uvāca
tataś cānu-dinaṁ dharmaḥ
satyaṁ śaucaṁ kṣamā dayā
kālena balinā rājan
naṅkṣyaty āyur balaṁ smṛtiḥ

TRANSLATION

Śukadeva Gosvāmī said: Then, O King, religion, truthfulness, cleanliness, tolerance, mercy, duration of life, physical strength and memory will all diminish day by day because of the powerful influence of the age of Kali.

PURPORT

During the present age, Kali-yuga, practically all desirable qualities will gradually diminish, as described in this verse. For example, *dharma,* which indicates a respect for higher authority that leads one to obey religious principles, will diminish.

In the Western world, theologians have been unable to scientifically present the laws of God or, indeed, God Himself, and thus in Western intellectual history a rigid dichotomy has arisen between theology and science. In an attempt to resolve this conflict, some theologians have agreed to modify their doctrines so that they conform not only to proven scientific facts but even to pseudoscientific speculations and hypotheses, which, though unproven, are hypocritically included within the realm of "science." On the other hand, some fanatical theologians disregard the scientific method altogether and insist on the veracity of their antiquated, sectarian dogmas.

Thus bereft of systematic Vedic theology, material science has moved into the destructive realm of gross materialism, while speculative Western philosophy has drifted into the superficiality of relativistic ethics and inconclusive linguistic analysis. With so many of the best Western minds dedicated to materialistic analysis, naturally much of Western religious life, separated from the intellectual mainstream, is dominated by irrational fanaticism and unauthorized mystic and mystery cults. People have become so ignorant of the science of God that they often lump the Kṛṣṇa consciousness movement in with this odd assortment of fanciful attempts at theology and religion. Thus *dharma,* or true religion, which is strict and conscious obedience to God's law, is diminishing.

Satyam, truthfulness, is also diminishing, simply because people do not know what the truth is. Without knowing the Absolute Truth, one cannot clearly understand the real significance or purpose of life merely by amassing huge quantities of relative or hypothetical truths.

Kṣamā, tolerance or forgiveness, is diminishing as well, because there is no practical method by which people can purify themselves and thus become free of envy. Unless one is purified by chanting the holy names of the Lord in an authorized program of spiritual improvement, the mind will be overwhelmed by anger, envy and all sorts of small-mindedness. Thus *dayā,* mercy, is also decreasing. All living beings are eternally connected by their common participation in the divine existence of God. When this existential oneness is obscured through atheism and agnosticism, people are not inclined to be merciful to one another; they cannot recognize their self-interest in promoting the welfare of other living beings. In fact, people are no longer even merciful to themselves: they systematically destroy themselves through liquor, drugs, tobacco, meat-eating, sexual promiscuity and whatever other cheap gratificatory processes are available to them.

Because of all these self-destructive practices and the powerful influence of time, the average life span (*āyur*) is decreasing. Modern scientists, seeking to gain credibility among the mass of people, often publish statistics supposedly showing that science has increased the average duration of life. But these statistics do not take into account the number of people killed through the cruel practice of abortion. When we figure aborted children into the life expectancy of the total population, we find that the average duration of life has not at all increased in the age of Kali but is rather decreasing drastically.

Balam, bodily strength, is also decreasing. The Vedic literature states that five thousand years ago, in the previous age, human beings—and even animals and plants—were larger and stronger. With the progress of the age of Kali, physical stature and strength will gradually diminish.

Certainly *smṛti,* memory, is weakening. In former ages human beings possessed superior memory, and they also did not encumber themselves with a terrible bureaucratic and technical society, as we have done. Thus essential information and abiding wisdom were preserved without recourse to writing. Of course, in the age of Kali things are dramatically different.

TEXT 2

vittam eva kalau nṛṇāṁ
janmācāra-guṇodayaḥ
dharma-nyāya-vyavasthāyāṁ
kāraṇaṁ balam eva hi

TRANSLATION

In Kali-yuga, wealth alone will be considered the sign of a man's good birth, proper behavior and fine qualities. And law and justice will be applied only on the basis of one's power.

PURPORT

In the age of Kali, a man is considered high class, middle class or low class merely according to his financial status, regardless of his knowledge, culture and behavior. In this age there are many great industrial and commercial cities with luxurious neighborhoods reserved for the wealthy. On beautiful tree-lined roads, within apparently aristocratic homes, it is not unusual to find many perverted, dishonest and sinful activities taking place. According to Vedic criteria, a man is considered high class if his behavior is enlightened, and his behavior is considered enlightened if his activities are dedicated to promoting the happiness of all creatures. Every living being is originally happy, because in all living bodies there is an eternal spiritual spark that partakes of the divine conscious nature of God. When our original spiritual awareness is revived, we become naturally blissful and satisfied in knowledge and peace. An enlightened, or educated, man should endeavor to revive his own spiritual understanding, and he should help others experience the same sublime consciousness.

The great Western philosopher Socrates stated that if a man is enlightened he will automatically act virtuously, and Śrīla Prabhupāda confirmed this fact. But in the Kali-yuga this obvious truth is disregarded, and the search for knowledge and virtue has been replaced by a vicious, animalistic competition for money. Those who prevail become the "top dogs" of modern society, and their consumer power grants them a reputation as most respectable, aristocratic and well educated.

This verse also states that in the age of Kali brute strength (*balam eva*) will determine law and "justice." We should keep in mind that in the progressive, Vedic culture, there was no artificial dichotomy between the spiritual and the public realms. All civilized people took it for granted that God is everywhere and that His laws are binding upon all creatures. The Sanskrit word *dharma,* therefore, indicates one's social, or public, obligation as well as one's religious duty. Thus responsibly caring for one's family is *dharma,* and engaging in the loving service of God is also *dharma*. This verse indicates, however, that in the age of Kali the principle of "might makes right" will hold sway.

In the First Chapter of this canto we observed how this principle infiltrated India's past. Similarly, as the Western world achieved political, economic and technological hegemony over Asian lands, bogus propaganda was disseminated to the effect that Indian, and in general all non-Western, religion, theology and philosophy are somehow primitive and unscientific—mere mythology and superstition. Fortunately this arrogant, irrational view is now dissipating, and people all over the world are beginning to appreciate the staggering wealth of spiritual philosophy and science available in the Sanskrit literature of India. In other words, many intelligent people no longer consider traditional Western religion or empirical science, which has virtually superseded religion as the official Western dogma, necessarily authoritative merely because the West has politically and economically subdued other geographic and ethnic configurations of humanity. Thus there is now hope that spiritual issues can be contested and resolved on a philosophical level and not merely by a crude test of arms.

Next this verse points out that the rule of law will be applied unequally to the powerful and the powerless. Already in many nations justice is available only to those who can pay and fight for it. In a civilized state, every man, woman and child must have equal and rapid access to a fair system of laws. In modern times we sometimes refer to this as human rights. Certainly human rights are one of the more obvious casualties of the age of Kali.

TEXT 3

dāmpatye'bhirucir hetur
māyaiva vyāvahārike
strītve puṁstve ca hi ratir
vipratve sūtram eva hi

TRANSLATION

Men and women will live together merely because of superficial attraction, and success in business will depend on deceit. Womanliness and manliness will be judged according to one's expertise in sex, and a man will be known as a *brāhmaṇa* just by his wearing a thread.

PURPORT

Just as human life as a whole has a great and serious purpose—namely spiritual liberation—fundamental human institutions such as marriage and child-rearing should also be dedicated to that great objective. Unfortunately, in the present age the satisfaction of the sex impulse has become the overriding, if not the exclusive, reason for marriage.

The sexual impulse, which induces the male and female of almost every species to combine physically, and in higher species also emotionally, is ultimately not a natural urge, because it is based on the unnatural identification of the self with the body. Life itself is a spiritual phenomenon. It is the soul that lives and gives apparent life to the biological machine called the body. Consciousness is the soul's manifest energy, and thus consciousness, awareness itself, is originally an entirely spiritual event. When life, or consciousness, is confined within a biological machine and falsely mistakes itself to be that machine, material existence occurs and sex desire arises.

God intends human life to be an opportunity for us to rectify this illusory mode of existence and return to the vast satisfaction of pure, godly existence. But because our identification with the material body is a long historical affair, it is difficult for most people to immediately break free from the demands of the materially molded mind. Therefore the Vedic scriptures prescribe sacred marriage, in which a so-called man and a so-called woman may combine in a regulated, spiritual marriage sheltered by overarching religious injunctions. In this way the candidate for self-realization who has selected family life can derive adequate satisfaction for his senses and simultaneously please the Lord within his heart by obeying religious injunctions. The Lord then purifies him of material desire.

In Kali-yuga this deep understanding has been almost lost, and, as stated in this verse, men and women combine like animals, solely on the basis of mutual attraction to bodies made of flesh, bone, membrane, blood and so on. In other words, in our modern, godless society the weak, superficial intelligence of humanity rarely penetrates beyond the gross physical covering of the eternal soul, and thus family life has in most cases lost its highest purpose and value.

A corollary point established in this verse is that in the age of Kali a woman is considered "a good woman" if she is sexually attractive and, indeed, sexually efficient. Similarly, a sexually attractive man is "a good man." The best example of this superficiality is the incredible attention twentieth-century people give to materialistic movie stars, music stars and other prominent figures in the entertainment industry. In fact, pursuing sexual experiences with various types of bodies is similar to drinking old wine from new bottles. But few people in the Kali-yuga can understand this.

Finally, this verse states that in the age of Kali a man will become known as a priest, or *brāhmaṇa,* merely by wearing ceremonial dress. In India, *brāhmaṇas* wear a sacred thread, and in other parts of world members of the priestly class have other ornaments and symbols. But in the age of Kali the symbols alone will suffice to establish a person as a religious leader, despite his ignorance of God.

TEXT 4

liṅgam evāśrama-khyātāv
anyonyāpatti-kāraṇam
avṛttyā nyāya-daurbalyaṁ
pāṇḍitye cāpalaṁ vacaḥ

TRANSLATION

A person's spiritual position will be ascertained merely according to external symbols, and on that same basis people will change from one spiritual order to the next. A person's propriety will be seriously questioned if he does not earn a good living. And one who is very clever at juggling words will be considered a learned scholar.

PURPORT

The previous verse stated that in the age of Kali the priestly class will be recognized by external symbols alone, and this verse extends the same principle to the other orders of society, namely the political or military class, the business or productive class, and finally the laborer or artisan class.

Modern sociologists have demonstrated that in those societies chiefly governed by the Protestant ethic, poverty is considered a sign of indolence, dirtiness, stupidity, immorality and worthlessness. In a God-conscious society, however, many persons voluntarily decide to dedicate their lives not to material acquisition but rather to the pursuit of knowledge and spirituality. Thus a preference for the simple and the austere may indicate intelligence, self-control and sensitivity to the higher purpose of life. Of course, in itself poverty does not establish these virtues, but it may sometimes be the result of them. In the Kali-yuga, however, this possibility is often forgotten.

Intellectuality is another casualty of the bewildering age of Kali. Modern so-called philosophers and scientists have created a technical, esoteric terminology for each branch of learning, and when they give lectures people consider them learned simply because of their ability to speak that which no one else can understand. In Western culture, the Greek Sophists were among the first to systematically argue for rhetoric and "efficiency" above wisdom and purity, and sophistry certainly flourishes in the twentieth century. Modern universities have very little wisdom, though they do possess a virtual infinity of technical data. Although many modern thinkers are fundamentally ignorant of the higher, spiritual reality, they are, so to speak, "good talkers," and most people simply don't notice their ignorance.

TEXT 5

anāḍhyataivāsādhutve
sādhutve dambha eva tu
svīkāra eva codvāhe
snānam eva prasādhanam

TRANSLATION

A person will be judged unholy if he does not have money, and hypocrisy will be accepted as virtue. Marriage will be arranged simply by verbal agreement, and a person will think he is fit to appear in public if he has merely taken a bath.

PURPORT

The word *dambha* indicates a self-righteous hypocrite—someone not so much concerned with *being* saintly as with *appearing* saintly. In the age of Kali there is a rather large number of self-righteous, hypocritical religious fanatics claiming to have the only way, the only truth and the only light. In many Muslim countries this mentality has resulted in brutal repression of religious freedom and thus destroyed the opportunity for enlightened spiritual dialectic. Fortunately, in much of the Western world there is a system of free religious expression. Even in the West, however, self-righteous hypocrites consider sincere and saintly followers of other disciplines to be heathens and devils.

Western religious fanatics are usually addicted to many bad habits, such as smoking, drinking, sex, gambling and animal slaughter. Although the followers of the Kṛṣṇa consciousness movement strictly avoid illicit sex, intoxication, gambling and animal-killing, and although they dedicate their lives to the constant glorification of God, self-righteous hypocrites claim that such strict austerity and devotion to God are "tricks of the devil." Thus the sinful are promoted as religious, and the saintly are decried as demonic. This pathetic incapacity to grasp the most rudimentary criteria of spirituality is a prominent symptom of Kali-yuga.

In this age, the institution of marriage will degenerate. Indeed, already a marriage certificate is sometimes cynically rejected as "a mere piece of paper." Forgetting the spiritual purpose of marriage and misunderstanding sex to be the goal of family life, lusty men and women directly engage in sexual affairs without the troublesome formalities and responsibilities of a legal relationship. Such foolish people argue that "sex is natural." But if sex is natural, pregnancy and childbirth are equally natural. And for the child it is certainly natural to be raised by a loving father and mother and in fact to have the same father and mother throughout his life. Psychological studies confirm that a child needs to be cared for by both his father and his mother, and thus it is obviously natural for sex to be accompanied by a permanent marriage arrangement. Hypocritical people justify unrestricted sex by saying "it is natural," but to avoid the natural consequence of sex—pregnancy—they use contraceptives, which certainly do not grow on trees. Indeed, contraceptives are not at all natural. Thus hypocrisy and foolishness abound in the age of Kali.

The verse concludes by saying that people will neglect to ornament their bodies properly in the present age. A human being should decorate his body with various religious ornaments. Vaiṣṇavas mark their bodies with *tilaka* blessed with the holy name of God. But in the age of Kali, religious and even material formalities are thoughtlessly discarded.

TEXT 6

dūre vāry-ayanaṁ tīrthaṁ
lāvaṇyaṁ keśa-dhāraṇam
udaraṁ-bharatā svārthaḥ
satyatve dhārṣṭyam eva hi

dākṣyaṁ kuṭumba-bharaṇaṁ
yaśo 'rthe dharma-sevanam

TRANSLATION

A sacred place will be taken to consist of no more than a reservoir of water located at a distance, and beauty will be thought to depend on one's hairstyle. Filling the belly will become the goal of life, and one who is audacious will be accepted as truthful. He who can maintain a family will be regarded as an expert man, and the principles of religion will be observed only for the sake of reputation.

PURPORT

In India there are many sacred places through which holy rivers flow. Foolish persons eagerly seek redemption from their sins by bathing in these rivers but do not take instruction from learned devotees of the Lord who reside in such places. One should go to a holy place seeking spiritual enlightenment and not just for ritualistic bathing.

In this age, people tirelessly arrange their hair in different styles, trying to enhance their facial beauty and sexuality. They do not know that actual beauty comes from within the heart, from the soul, and that only a person who is pure is truly attractive. As the difficulties of this age increase, filling one's belly will be the mark of success, and one who can maintain his own family will be considered brilliant in economic affairs. Religion will be practiced, if at all, only for the sake of reputation and without any essential understanding of the Supreme Personality of Godhead.

TEXT 7

evaṁ prajābhir duṣṭābhir
ākīrṇe kṣiti-maṇḍale
brahma-viṭ-kṣatra-śūdrāṇāṁ
yo balī bhavitā nṛpaḥ

TRANSLATION

As the earth thus becomes crowded with a corrupt population, whoever among any of the social classes shows himself to be the strongest will gain political power.

TEXT 8

prajā hi lubdhai rājanyair
nirghṛṇair dasyu-dharmabhiḥ
ācchinna-dāra-draviṇā
yāsyanti giri-kānanam

TRANSLATION

Losing their wives and properties to such avaricious and merciless rulers, who will behave no better than ordinary thieves, the citizens will flee to the mountains and forests.

TEXT 9

śāka-mūlāmiṣa-kṣaudra-
phala-puṣpāṣṭi-bhojanāḥ
anāvṛṣṭyā vinaṅkṣyanti
durbhikṣa-kara-pīḍitāḥ

TRANSLATION

Harassed by famine and excessive taxes, people will resort to eating leaves, roots, flesh, wild honey, fruits, flowers and seeds. Struck by drought, they will become completely ruined.

PURPORT

Śrīmad-Bhāgavatam authoritatively describes the future of our planet. Just as a leaf disconnected from a plant or tree dries up, withers and disintegrates, when human society is disconnected from the Supreme Lord it withers up and disintegrates in violence and chaos. Despite our computers and rockets, if the Supreme Lord does not send rain we shall all starve.

TEXT 10

śīta-vātātapa-prāvṛḍ-
himair anyonyataḥ prajāḥ
kṣut-tṛḍbhyāṁ vyādhibhiś caiva
santapsyante ca cintayā

TRANSLATION

The citizens will suffer greatly from cold, wind, heat, rain and snow. They will be further tormented by quarrels, hunger, thirst, disease and severe anxiety.

TEXT 11

triṁśad viṁśati varṣāṇi
paramāyuḥ kalau nṛṇām

TRANSLATION

The maximum duration of life for human beings in Kali-yuga will become fifty years.

TEXTS 12–16

kṣīyamāṇeṣu deheṣu
dehināṁ kali-doṣataḥ
varṇāśramavatāṁ dharme
naṣṭe veda-pathe nṛṇām
pāṣaṇḍa-pracure dharme
dasyu-prāyeṣu rājasu
cauryānṛta-vṛthā-hiṁsā-
nānā-vṛttiṣu vai nṛṣu

śūdra-prāyeṣu varṇeṣu
cchāga-prāyāsu dhenuṣu
gṛha-prāyeṣv āśrameṣu
yauna-prāyeṣu bandhuṣu
aṇu-prāyāsv oṣadhīṣu
śamī-prāyeṣu sthāsnuṣu
vidyut-prāyeṣu megheṣu
śūnya-prāyeṣu sadmasu
itthaṁ kalau gata-prāye
janeṣu khara-dharmiṣu
dharma-trāṇāya sattvena
bhagavān avatariṣyati

TRANSLATION

By the time the age of Kali ends, the bodies of all creatures will be greatly reduced in size, and the religious principles of followers of *varṇāśrama* will be ruined. The path of the *Vedas* will be completely forgotten in human society, and so-called religion will be mostly atheistic. The kings will mostly be thieves, the occupations of men will be stealing, lying and needless violence, and all the social classes will be reduced to the lowest level of *śūdras*. Cows will be like goats, spiritual hermitages will be no different from mundane houses, and family ties will extend no further than the immediate bonds of marriage. Most plants and herbs will be tiny, and all trees will appear like dwarf *śamī* trees. Clouds will be full of lightning, homes will be devoid of piety, and all human beings will have become like asses. At that time, the Supreme Personality of Godhead will appear on the earth. Acting with the power of pure spiritual goodness, He will rescue eternal religion.

PURPORT

Significantly, these verses point out that most so-called religions in this age will be atheistic (*pāsaṇḍa-pracure dharme*). In confirmation of the *Bhāgavatam's* prediction, the United States Supreme Court has recently ruled that to be considered a religion a system of belief need not recognize a supreme being. Also, many atheistic, voidistic belief systems, often imported from the Orient, have attracted the attention of modern atheistic scientists, who expound on the similarities between Eastern and Western voidism in fashionable, esoteric books.

These verses vividly describe many unsavory symptoms of the age of Kali. Ultimately, at the end of this age, Lord Kṛṣṇa will descend as Kalki and remove the thoroughly demonic persons from the face of the earth.

TEXT 17

carācara-guror viṣṇor
īśvarasyākhilātmanaḥ
dharma-trāṇāya sādhūnāṁ
janma karmāpanuttaye

TRANSLATION

Lord Viṣṇu—the Supreme Personality of Godhead, the spiritual master of all moving and nonmoving living beings, and the Supreme Soul of all—takes birth to protect the principles of religion and to relieve His saintly devotees from the reactions of material work.

TEXT 18

śambhala-grāma-mukhyasya
brāhmaṇasya mahātmanaḥ

bhavane viṣṇuyaśasaḥ
kalkiḥ prādurbhaviṣyati

TRANSLATION

Lord Kalki will appear in the home of the most eminent *brāhmaṇa* of Śambhala village, the great soul Viṣṇuyaśā.

TEXTS 19–20

aśvam āśu-gam āruhya
devadattaṁ jagat-patiḥ
asināsādhu-damanam
aṣṭaiśvarya-guṇānvitaḥ
vicarann āśunā kṣauṇyāṁ
hayenāpratima-dyutiḥ
nṛpa-liṅga-cchado dasyūn
koṭiśo nihaniṣyati

TRANSLATION

Lord Kalki, the Lord of the universe, will mount His swift horse Devadatta and, sword in hand, travel over the earth exhibiting His eight mystic opulences and eight special qualities of Godhead. Displaying His unequaled effulgence and riding with great speed, He will kill by the millions those thieves who have dared dress as kings.

PURPORT

These verses describe the thrilling pastimes of Lord Kalki. Anyone would be attracted by the sight of a powerful, beautiful man riding on a wonderful horse at lightning speed, chastising and devastating cruel, demonic people with the sword in His hand.

Of course, fanatical materialists may argue that this picture of Lord Kalki is a mere anthropomorphic creation of the human mind—a mythological deity created by people who need to believe in some superior being. But this argument is not logical, nor does it prove anything. It is merely the opinion of certain people. We need water, but that does not mean man creates water. We also need food, oxygen and many other things that we do not create. Since our general experience is that our needs correspond to available objects existing in the external world, that we appear to need a Supreme Lord would tend to indicate that in fact there is a Supreme Lord. In other words, nature endows us with a sense of need for things that actually exist and that are in fact necessary for our well-being. Similarly, we experience a need for God because we are in fact part of God and cannot live without Him. At the end of Kali-yuga this same God will appear as the mighty Kalki *avatāra* and beat the pollution out of the demons.

TEXT 21

atha teṣāṁ bhaviṣyanti
manāṁsi viśadāni vai
vāsudevāṅga-rāgāti-
puṇya-gandhānila-spṛśām
paura-jānapadānāṁ vai
hateṣv akhila-dasyuṣu

TRANSLATION

After all the impostor kings have been killed, the residents of the cities and towns will feel the breezes carrying the most sacred fragrance of the sandalwood paste and other decorations of Lord Vāsudeva, and their minds will thereby become transcendentally pure.

PURPORT

Nothing can surpass the sublime experience of being dramatically rescued by a great hero who happens to be the Supreme Lord. The death of the demons at the end of Kali-yuga is accompanied by fragrant spiritual breezes, and thus the atmosphere becomes most enchanting.

TEXT 22

teṣāṁ prajā-visargaś ca
sthaviṣṭhaḥ sambhaviṣyati
vāsudeve bhagavati
sattva-mūrtau hṛdi sthite

TRANSLATION

When Lord Vāsudeva, the Supreme Personality of Godhead, appears in their hearts in His transcendental form of goodness, the remaining citizens will abundantly repopulate the earth.

TEXT 23

yadāvatīrṇo bhagavān
kalkir dharma-patir hariḥ
kṛtaṁ bhaviṣyati tadā
prajā-sūtiś ca sāttvikī

TRANSLATION

When the Supreme Lord has appeared on earth as Kalki, the maintainer of religion, Satya-yuga will begin, and human society will bring forth progeny in the mode of goodness.

TEXT 24

yadā candraś ca sūryaś ca
tathā tiṣya-bṛhaspatī
eka-rāśau sameṣyanti
bhaviṣyati tadā kṛtam

TRANSLATION

When the moon, the sun and Bṛhaspatī are together in the constellation Karkaṭa, and all three enter simultaneously into the lunar mansion Puṣyā—at that exact moment the age of Satya, or Kṛta, will begin.

TEXT 25

ye 'tītā vartamānā ye
bhaviṣyanti ca pārthivāḥ
te ta uddeśataḥ proktā
vaṁśīyāḥ soma-sūryayoḥ

TRANSLATION

Thus I have described all the kings—past, present and future—who belong to the dynasties of the sun and the moon.

TEXT 26

ārabhya bhavato janma
yāvan nandābhiṣecanam
etad varṣa-sahasraṁ tu
śataṁ pañcadaśottaram

TRANSLATION

From your birth up to the coronation of King Nanda, 1,150 years will pass.

PURPORT

Although Śukadeva Gosvāmī previously described approximately fifteen hundred years of royal dynasties, it is understood that some overlapping occurred between kings. Therefore the present chronological calculation should be taken as authoritative.

TEXTS 27–28

saptarṣīṇāṁ tu yau pūrvau
dṛśyete uditau divi
tayos tu madhye nakṣatraṁ
dṛśyate yat samaṁ niśi

tenaiva ṛṣayo yuktās
tiṣṭhanty abda-śataṁ nṛṇām
te tvadīye dvijāḥ kāla
adhunā cāśritā maghāḥ

TRANSLATION

Of the seven stars forming the constellation of the seven sages, Pulaha and Kratu are the first to rise in the night sky. If a line running north and south were drawn through their midpoint, whichever of the lunar mansions this line passes through is said to be the ruling asterism of the constellation for that time. The Seven Sages will remain connected with that particular lunar mansion for one hundred human years. Currently, during your lifetime, they are situated in the *nakṣatra* called Maghā.

TEXT 29

viṣṇor bhagavato bhānuḥ
kṛṣṇākhyo 'sau divaṁ gataḥ
tadāviśat kalir lokaṁ
pāpe yad ramate janaḥ

TRANSLATION

The Supreme Lord, Viṣṇu, is brilliant like the sun and is known as Kṛṣṇa. When He returned to the spiritual sky, Kali entered this world, and people then began to take pleasure in sinful activities.

TEXT 30

yāvat sa pāda-padmābhyāṁ
spṛśan āste ramā-patiḥ
tāvat kalir vai pṛthivīṁ
parākrantuṁ na cāśakat

TRANSLATION

As long as Lord Śrī Kṛṣṇa, the husband of the goddess of fortune, touched the earth with His lotus feet, Kali was powerless to subdue this planet.

PURPORT

Although even during the time of Lord Kṛṣṇa's presence on earth Kali had entered the earth to a slight extent through the impious activities of Duryodhana and his allies, Lord Kṛṣṇa consistently suppressed Kali's influence. Kali could not flourish until Lord Kṛṣṇa had left the earth.

TEXT 31

yadā devarṣayaḥ sapta
maghāsu vicaranti hi
tadā pravṛttas tu kalir
dvādaśābda-śatātmakaḥ

TRANSLATION

When the constellation of the seven sages is passing through the lunar mansion Maghā, the age of Kali begins. It comprises twelve hundred *years of the demigods.**

TEXT 32

yadā maghābhyo yāsyanti
pūrvāṣāḍhāṁ maharṣayaḥ
tadā nandāt prabhṛty eṣa
kalir vṛddhiṁ gamiṣyati

***Note:** *One year of the demigods is equal to 360 years of humankind.*

TRANSLATION

When the great sages of the Saptarṣi constellation pass from Maghā to Pūrvāsāḍhā, Kali will have his full strength, beginning from King Nanda and his dynasty.

TEXT 33

yasmin kṛṣṇo divaṁ yātas
tasminn eva tadāhani
pratipannaṁ kali-yugam
iti prāhuḥ purā-vidaḥ

TRANSLATION

Those who scientifically understand the past declare that on the very day that Lord Śrī Kṛṣṇa departed for the spiritual world, the influence of the age of Kali began.

PURPORT

Although technically Kali-yuga was to begin during the time of Lord Kṛṣṇa's presence on earth, this fallen age had to wait meekly for the departure of the Supreme Personality of Godhead.

TEXT 34

divyābdānāṁ sahasrānte
caturthe tu punaḥ kṛtam
bhaviṣyati tadā nṛṇāṁ
mana ātma-prakāśakam

TRANSLATION

After the one thousand celestial years of Kali-yuga, the Satya-yuga will manifest again. At that time the minds of all men will become self-effulgent.

TEXT 35

ity eṣa mānavo vaṁśo
yathā saṅkhyāyate bhuvi
tathā viṭ-śūdra-viprāṇāṁ
tās tā jñeyā yuge yuge

TRANSLATION

Thus I have described the royal dynasty of Manu, as it is known on this earth. One can similarly study the history of the *vaiśyas*, *śūdras* and *brāhmaṇas* living in the various ages.

PURPORT

Just as the dynasty of kings includes exalted and insignificant, virtuous and wicked monarchs, varieties of human character are found in the intellectual, commercial and laboring orders of society.

TEXT 36

eteṣāṁ nāma-liṅgānāṁ
puruṣāṇāṁ mahātmanām
kathā-mātrāvaśiṣṭānāṁ
kīrtir eva sthitā bhuvi

TRANSLATION

These personalities, who were great souls, are now known only by their names. They exist only in accounts from the past, and only their fame remains on the earth.

PURPORT

Although one may consider oneself to be a great, powerful leader, he will ultimately end up as a name in a long list of names. In other words, it is useless to be attached to power and position in the material world.

TEXT 37

devāpiḥ śāntanor bhrātā
maruś cekṣvāku-vaṁśa-jaḥ
kalāpa-grāma āsāte
mahā-yoga-balānvitau

TRANSLATION

Devāpi, the brother of Mahārāja Śāntanu, and Maru, the descendant of Ikṣvāku, both possess great mystic strength and are living even now in the village of Kalāpa.

TEXT 38

tāv ihaitya kaler ante
vāsudevānuśikṣitau
varṇāśrama-yutaṁ dharmaṁ
pūrva-vat prathayiṣyataḥ

TRANSLATION

At the end of the age of Kali, these two kings, having received instruction directly from the Supreme Personality of Godhead, Vāsudeva, will return to human society and reestablish the eternal religion of man, characterized by the divisions of *varṇa* and *āśrama*, just as it was before.

PURPORT

According to this and the previous verse, the two great kings who will reestablish human culture after the end of Kali-yuga have already descended to the earth, where they are patiently waiting to render their devotional service to Lord Viṣṇu.

TEXT 39

kṛtaṁ tretā dvāparaṁ ca
kaliś ceti catur-yugam

anena krama-yogena
bhuvi prāṇiṣu vartate

TRANSLATION

The cycle of four ages—Satya, Tretā, Dvāpara and Kali—continues perpetually among living beings on this earth, repeating the same general sequence of events.

TEXT 40

rājann ete mayā proktā
nara-devās tathāpare
bhūmau mamatvaṁ kṛtvānte
hitvemāṁ nidhanaṁ gatāḥ

TRANSLATION

My dear King Parīkṣit, all these kings I have described, as well as all other human beings, come to this earth and stake their claims, but ultimately they all must give up this world and meet their destruction.

TEXT 41

kṛmi-viḍ-bhasma-saṁjñānte
rāja-nāmno 'pi yasya ca
bhūta-dhruk tat-kṛte svārthaṁ
kiṁ veda nirayo yataḥ

TRANSLATION

Even though a person's body may now have the designation "king," in the end its name will be "worms," "stool" or "ashes." What can a person who injures other living beings for the sake of his body know about his own self-interest, since his activities are simply leading him to hell?

PURPORT

After death, the body may be buried and eaten by worms, or it may be thrown in the street or forest to be eaten by animals who will pass out its remnants as stool, or it may be burned and converted into ashes. Therefore one should not pave his way to hell by using his temporary body to injure the bodies of other living beings. In this verse the word *bhūta* includes nonhuman life forms, who are also creatures of God. One should give up all envious violence and learn to see God in everything by the process of Kṛṣṇa consciousness.

TEXT 42

kathaṁ seyam akhaṇḍā bhūḥ
pūrvair me puruṣair dhṛtā
mat-putrasya ca pautrasya
mat-pūrvā vaṁśa-jasya vā

TRANSLATION

[The materialistic king thinks:] "This unbounded earth was held by my predecessors and is now under my sovereignty. How can I arrange for it to remain in the hands of my sons, grandsons and other descendants?"

PURPORT

This is an example of foolish possessiveness.

TEXT 43

tejo-'b-anna-mayaṁ kāyaṁ
gṛhītvātmatayābudhāḥ
mahīṁ mamatayā cobhau
hitvānte 'darśanaṁ gatāḥ

TRANSLATION

Although the foolish accept the body made of earth, water and fire as "me" and this earth as "mine," in every case they have ultimately abandoned both their body and the earth and passed away into oblivion.

PURPORT

Although the soul is eternal, our so-called family tradition and earthly fame will certainly pass into oblivion.

TEXT 44

ye ye bhū-patayo rājan
bhuñjate bhuvam ojasā
kālena te kṛtāḥ sarve
kathā-mātrāḥ kathāsu ca

TRANSLATION

My dear King Parīkṣit, all these kings who tried to enjoy the earth by their strength were reduced by the force of time to nothing more than historical accounts.

PURPORT

The word *rājan,* "O King," is significant in this verse. Parīkṣit Mahārāja was preparing to give up his body and go back home, back to Godhead, and Śukadeva Gosvāmī, his most merciful spiritual master, devastated any possible attachment that he might have to the position of king by showing the ultimate insignificance of such a position. By the causeless mercy of the spiritual master one is prepared to go back home, back to Godhead. The spiritual master teaches one to relax one's strong grip on material illusion and leave the kingdom of *māyā* behind. Although Śukadeva Gosvāmī speaks very bluntly within this chapter about the so-called glory of the material world, he is exhibiting the causeless mercy of the spiritual master, who takes his surrendered disciple back to the kingdom of Godhead, Vaikuṇṭha.

CHAPTER 2

Śrīmad-Bhāgavatam, Canto Twelve, Chapter Three

"The Bhūmi-gītā"

This chapter describes how the earth took note of the foolishness of the many kings bent on conquering her. It also describes how even though the age of Kali is full of faults, the glorification of the name of Lord Hari destroys them all.

Great kings, who are actually just playthings of death, desire to subdue their six internal enemies—the five senses and the mind—and afterward they imagine they will go on to conquer the earth and all its oceans. Seeing their false hopes, the earth simply laughs, for eventually they all must leave this planet and go elsewhere, as have all the great kings and monarchs of the past. Moreover, after usurping the earth or some part of it—which is actually unconquerable and must in every case be given up—fathers, sons, brothers, friends and relatives quarrel over it.

Thus the study of history naturally leads to the conclusion that all worldly achievements are temporary, and this conclusion should give rise to a sense of renunciation. Ultimately, the highest goal of life for any living entity is pure devotion to Lord Kṛṣṇa, which annihilates all inauspiciousness. In the age of Satya, religion was complete, still possessing its four legs of truth, mercy, austerity and charity. With the coming of each succeeding age, starting with Tretā, these religious qualities each diminish by one quarter. In Kali-yuga the legs of religion retain only one fourth of their power, and even that will be lost with the progress of the age. The mode of goodness is predominant during Satya-yuga, and the mode of passion is predominant during the Tretā-yuga. The mixed modes of passion and ignorance are predominant during Dvāpara-yuga, and in the age of Kali the mode of ignorance is predominant. Atheism, the smallness and inferiority of all things, and devotion to the genitals and belly are very much evident in the age of Kali. Living entities contaminated by the influence of Kali do not worship the Supreme Lord, Śrī Hari, even though they can be freed from all bondage and easily achieve the supreme destination simply by chanting the glories of His name and taking shelter of Him. But if somehow or other the Supreme Personality of Godhead becomes manifest within the hearts of the conditioned souls in Kali-yuga, then all faults of place, time and personality inherent in the age will be destroyed. Kali-yuga is an ocean of faults, but it possesses one great quality: simply by the chanting of the name of Kṛṣṇa, one can be delivered from material association and attain the Absolute Truth. All that was accomplished in the age of Satya by meditation, in the age of Tretā by sacrificial performances and in the age of Dvāpara by temple worship is easily gained during the Kali-yuga by the simple process of *hari-kīrtana.*

TEXT 1

śrī-śuka uvāca
dṛṣṭvātmani jaye vyagrān
nṛpān hasati bhūr iyam
aho mā vijigīṣanti
mṛtyoḥ krīḍanakā nṛpāḥ

TRANSLATION

Śukadeva Gosvāmī said: Seeing the kings of this earth busy trying to conquer her, the earth herself laughed. She said: "Just see how these kings, who are actually playthings in the hands of death, are desiring to conquer me.

TEXT 2

kāma eṣa narendrāṇāṁ
moghaḥ syād viduṣām api
yena phenopame piṇḍe
ye 'ti-viśrambhitā nṛpāḥ

TRANSLATION

"Great rulers of men, even those who are learned, meet frustration and failure because of material lust. Driven by lust, these kings place great hope and faith in the dead lump of flesh called the body, even though the material frame is as fleeting as bubbles of foam on water.

TEXTS 3–4

pūrvaṁ nirjitya ṣaḍ-vargaṁ
jeṣyāmo rāja-mantriṇaḥ
tataḥ saciva-paurāpta-
karīndrān asya kaṇṭakān
evaṁ krameṇa jeṣyāmaḥ
pṛthvīṁ sāgara-mekhalām
ity āśā-baddha-hṛdayā
na paśyanty antike 'ntakam

TRANSLATION

"Kings and politicians imagine: 'First I will conquer my senses and mind; then I will subdue my chief ministers and rid myself of the thorn-pricks of my advisors, citizens, friends and relatives, as well as the keepers of my elephants. In this way I will gradually conquer the entire earth.' Because the hearts of these leaders are bound by great expectations, they fail to see death waiting nearby.

PURPORT

To satisfy their greed for power, determined politicians, dictators and military leaders undergo severe austerities and sacrifice, with much self-discipline. Then they lead their great nations in a struggle to control the sea, land, air and space. Although the politicians and their followers will soon be dead—since birth and death are all inevitable in this world—they persist in their frenetic struggle for ephemeral glory.

TEXT 5

samudrāvaraṇāṁ jitvā
māṁ viśanty abdhim ojasā
kiyad ātma-jayasyaitan
muktir ātma-jaye phalam

TRANSLATION

"After conquering all the land on my surface, these proud kings forcibly enter the ocean to conquer the sea itself. What is the use of their self-control, which is aimed at political exploitation? The actual goal of self-control is spiritual liberation."

TEXT 6

yāṁ visṛjyaiva manavas
tat-sutāś ca kurūdvaha
gatā yathāgataṁ yuddhe
tāṁ māṁ jeṣyanty abuddhayaḥ

TRANSLATION

O best of the Kurus, the earth continued as follows: "Although in the past great men and their descendants have left me, departing from this world in the same helpless way they came into it, even today foolish men are trying to conquer me.

TEXT 7

mat-kṛte pitṛ-putrāṇāṁ
bhrātṝṇāṁ cāpi vigrahaḥ
jāyate hy asatāṁ rājye
mamatā-baddha-cetasām

TRANSLATION

"For the sake of conquering me, materialistic persons fight one another. Fathers oppose their sons, and brothers fight one another, because their hearts are bound to possessing political power.

TEXT 8

mamaiveyaṁ mahī kṛtsnā
na te mūḍheti vādinaḥ
spardhamānā mitho ghnanti
mriyante mat-kṛte nṛpāḥ

TRANSLATION

"Political leaders challenge one another: 'All this land is mine! It's not yours, you fool!' Thus they attack one another and die.

PURPORT

This verse describes with brilliant clarity the mundane political mentality that provokes innumerable conflicts in the world. For example, as we prepare this translation of *Śrīmad-Bhāgavatam,* British and Argentine military forces are bitterly fighting over the tiny Falkland Islands.

The fact is that the Supreme Lord is the proprietor of all land. Of course, even in a God-conscious world political boundaries exist. But in such a God-conscious atmosphere political tensions are greatly eased, and people of all lands welcome each other and respect each other's right to live in peace.

TEXTS 9–13

pṛthuḥ purūravā gādhir
nahuṣo bharato 'rjunaḥ
māndhātā sagaro rāmaḥ
khaṭvāṅgo dhundhuhā raghuḥ
tṛṇabindur yayātiś ca
śaryātiḥ śantanur gayaḥ
bhagīrathaḥ kuvalayāśvaḥ
kakutstho naiṣadho nṛgaḥ
hiraṇyakaśipur vṛtro
rāvaṇo loka-rāvaṇaḥ
namuciḥ śambaro bhaumo
hiraṇyākṣo 'tha tārakaḥ
anye ca bahavo daityā
rājāno ye maheśvarāḥ
sarve sarva-vidaḥ śūrāḥ
sarve sarva-jito 'jitāḥ
mamatāṁ mayy avartanta
kṛtvoccair martya-dharmiṇaḥ
kathāvaśeṣāḥ kālena
hy akṛtārthāḥ kṛtā vibho

TRANSLATION

"Such kings as Pṛthu, Purūravā, Gādhi, Nahuṣa, Bharata, Kārtavīrya Arjuna, Māndhātā, Sagara, Rāma, Khaṭvāṅga, Dhundhuhā, Raghu, Tṛṇabindu, Yayāti, Śaryāti, Śantanu, Gaya, Bhagīratha, Kuvalayāśva, Kakutstha, Naiṣadha, Nṛga, Hiraṇyakaśipu, Vṛtra, Rāvaṇa, who made the whole world lament, Namuci, Śambara, Bhauma, Hiraṇyākṣa and Tāraka, as well as many other demons and kings who possessed great powers of control over others, were all full of knowledge, heroic, all-conquering and unconquerable. Nevertheless, O almighty Lord, although they lived their lives intensely trying to possess me, these kings were subject to the passage of time, which reduced them all to mere historical accounts. None of them could permanently establish their rule."

PURPORT

According to Śrīla Śrīdhara Svāmī, and as confirmed by Śrīla Viśvanātha Cakravartī Ṭhākura, the King Rāma mentioned here is not the incarnation of Godhead Rāmacandra. Pṛthu Mahārāja is understood to be an incarnation of the Supreme Personality of Godhead who completely exhibited the characteristics of an earthly king, claiming proprietorship over the entire earth. A saintly king like Pṛthu Mahārāja, however, controls the earth on behalf of the Supreme Personality of Godhead, whereas a demon such as Hiraṇyakaśipu or Rāvaṇa tries to exploit the earth for his personal sense gratification. Nevertheless, both saintly kings and demons must leave the earth. In this way their political supremacy is ultimately neutralized by the force of time.

Modern political leaders cannot even temporarily control the entire earth, nor are their opulences and intelligence unlimited. Possessing hopelessly fragmented power, enjoying a minuscule life span, and lacking deep existential intelligence, modern leaders inevitably are symbols of frustration and misdirected ambition.

TEXT 14

kathā imās te kathitā mahīyasāṁ
vitāya lokeṣu yaśaḥ pareyuṣām
vijñāna-vairāgya-vivakṣayā vibho
vaco-vibhūtīr na tu pāramārthyam

TRANSLATION

Śukadeva Gosvāmī said: O mighty Parīkṣit, I have related to you the narrations of all these great kings, who spread their fame throughout the world and then departed. My real purpose was to teach transcendental knowledge and renunciation. Stories of kings lend power and opulence to these narrations but do not in themselves constitute the ultimate aspect of knowledge.

PURPORT

Since all the narrations of *Śrīmad-Bhāgavatam* bring the reader to the perfection of transcendental knowledge, they all give supreme spiritual lessons though apparently dealing with kings or other mundane subject matter. In relation with Kṛṣṇa, all ordinary topics become transcendental narrations, with the power to bring the reader to the perfection of life.

TEXT 15

yas tūttamaḥ-śloka-guṇānuvādaḥ
saṅgīyate 'bhīkṣṇam amaṅgala-ghnaḥ
tam eva nityaṁ śṛṇuyād abhīkṣṇaṁ
kṛṣṇe 'malāṁ bhaktim abhīpsamānaḥ

TRANSLATION

The person who desires pure devotional service to Lord Kṛṣṇa should hear the narrations of Lord Uttamaḥśloka's glorious qualities, the constant chanting of which destroys everything inauspicious. The devotee should engage in such listening in regular daily assemblies and should also continue his hearing throughout the day.

PURPORT

Since any topic related to Lord Kṛṣṇa is auspicious and transcendental, the direct narration of Lord Kṛṣṇa's own activities, political and nonpolitical, is certainly the supreme subject matter for hearing. The word *nityam* here indicates regulated cultivation of the topics of Lord Kṛṣṇa, and *abhīkṣṇam* indicates constant remembrance of such regulated spiritual experiences.

TEXT 16

śrī-rājovāca
kenopāyena bhagavan
kaler doṣān kalau janāḥ
vidhamiṣyanty upacitāṁs
tan me brūhi yathā mune

TRANSLATION

King Parīkṣit said: My lord, how can persons living in the age of Kali rid themselves of the cumulative contamination of this age? O great sage, please explain this to me.

PURPORT

King Parīkṣit was a compassionate, saintly ruler. Thus, after hearing of the abominable qualities of the age of Kali, he naturally inquired as to how those born in this age can free themselves of its inherent contamination.

TEXT 17

yugāni yuga-dharmāṁś ca
mānaṁ pralaya-kalpayoḥ

kālasyeśvara-rūpasya
gatiṁ viṣṇor mahātmanaḥ

TRANSLATION

Please explain the different ages of universal history, the special qualities of each age, the duration of cosmic maintenance and destruction, and the movement of time, which is the direct representation of the Supreme Soul, the Personality of Godhead, Lord Viṣṇu.

TEXT 18

śrī-śuka uvāca
kṛte pravartate dharmaś
catuṣ-pāt taj-janair dhṛtaḥ
satyaṁ dayā tapo dānam
iti pādā vibhor nṛpa

TRANSLATION

Śukadeva Gosvāmī said: My dear King, in the beginning, during Satya-yuga, the age of truth, religion is present with all four of its legs intact and is carefully maintained by the people of that age. These four legs of powerful religion are truthfulness, mercy, austerity and charity.

PURPORT

Just as there are four seasons, there are four ages of the earth, each lasting hundreds of thousands of years. The first of these is Satya-yuga, when such good qualities as charity are prominent.

Actual charity, here referred to as *dānam,* is to award fearlessness and freedom to others, not to give them some material means of temporary pleasure or relief. Any material "charitable" arrangement will inevitably be crushed by the onward march of time. Thus only realization of one's eternal existence beyond the reach of time can make one fearless, and only freedom from material desire constitutes real freedom, for it enables one to escape the bondage of the laws of nature. Therefore real charity is to help people revive their eternal, spiritual consciousness.

Religion is here referred to as *vibhu,* "the mighty," because universal religious principles are not different from the Supreme Lord Himself and ultimately lead one to His kingdom. The qualities mentioned here—truthfulness, mercy, austerity and charity—are universal, nonsectarian aspects of pious life.

In the First Canto of *Śrīmad-Bhāgavatam,* the fourth leg of religion is listed as cleanliness. According to Śrīla Viśvanātha Cakravartī Ṭhākura, this is an alternative definition of the word *dānam* in the present context.

TEXT 19

santuṣṭāḥ karuṇā maitrāḥ
śāntā dāntās titikṣavaḥ
ātmārāmāḥ sama-dṛśaḥ
prāyaśaḥ śramaṇā janāḥ

TRANSLATION

The people of Satya-yuga are for the most part self-satisfied, merciful, friendly to all, peaceful, sober and tolerant. They take their pleasure from within, see all things equally and always endeavor diligently for spiritual perfection.

PURPORT

Sama-darśana, equal vision, is based on the perception of the Supreme Spirit behind all material variety and within all living entities.

TEXT 20

tretāyāṁ dharma-pādānāṁ
turyāṁśo hīyate śanaiḥ

adharma-pādair anṛta-
hiṁṣāsantoṣa-vigrahaiḥ

TRANSLATION

In Tretā-yuga each leg of religion is gradually reduced by one quarter by the influence of the four pillars of irreligion—lying, violence, dissatisfaction and quarrel.

PURPORT

By falsity truth is diminished, by violence mercy is diminished, by dissatisfaction austerity is diminished, and by quarrel charity and cleanliness are diminished.

TEXT 21

tadā kriyā-tapo-niṣṭhā
nāti-hiṁsrā na lampaṭāḥ
trai-vargikās trayī-vṛddhā
varṇā brahmottarā nṛpa

TRANSLATION

In the Tretā age people are devoted to ritual performances and severe austerities. They are not excessively violent or very lusty after sensual pleasure. Their interest lies primarily in religiosity, economic development and regulated sense gratification, and they achieve prosperity by following the prescriptions of the three *Vedas*. Although in this age society evolves into four separate classes, O King, most people are *brāhmaṇas*.

TEXT 22

tapaḥ-satya-dayā-dāneṣv
ardhaṁ hrasvati dvāpare
hiṁsātuṣṭy-anṛta-dveṣair
dharmasyādharma-lakṣaṇaiḥ

TRANSLATION

In Dvāpara-yuga the religious qualities of austerity, truth, mercy and charity are reduced to one half by their irreligious counterparts—dissatisfaction, untruth, violence and enmity.

TEXT 23

yaśasvino mahā-śīlāḥ
svādhyāyādhyayane ratāḥ
āḍhyāḥ kuṭumbino hṛṣṭā
varṇāḥ kṣatra-dvijottarāḥ

TRANSLATION

In the Dvāpara age people are interested in glory and are very noble. They devote themselves to the study of the Vedas, possess great opulence, support large families and enjoy life with vigor. Of the four classes, the kṣatriyas and brāhmaṇas are most numerous.

TEXT 24

kalau tu dharma-pādānāṁ
turyāṁśo 'dharma-hetubhiḥ
edhamānaiḥ kṣīyamāṇo
hy ante so 'pi vinaṅkṣyati

TRANSLATION

In the age of Kali only one fourth of the religious principles remains. That last remnant will continuously be decreased by the ever-increasing principles of irreligion and will finally be destroyed.

TEXT 25

tasmin lubdhā durācārā
nirdayāḥ śuṣka-vairiṇaḥ
durbhagā bhūri-tarṣāś ca
śūdra-dāsottarāḥ prajāḥ

TRANSLATION

In the Kali age people tend to be greedy, ill-behaved and merciless, and they fight one another without good reason. Unfortunate and obsessed with material desires, the people of Kali-yuga are almost all *śūdras* and barbarians.

PURPORT

In this age, we can already observe that most people are laborers, clerks, fishermen, artisans or other kinds of workers within the *śūdra* category. Enlightened devotees of God and noble political leaders are extremely scarce, and even independent businessmen and farmers are a vanishing breed as huge business conglomerates increasingly convert them into subservient employees. Vast regions of the earth are already populated by barbarians and semibarbarous peoples, making the entire situation dangerous and bleak. The Kṛṣṇa consciousness movement is empowered to rectify the current dismal state of affairs. It is the only hope for the ghastly age called Kali-yuga.

TEXT 26

sattvaṁ rajas tama iti
dṛśyante puruṣe guṇāḥ
kāla-sañcoditās te vai
parivartanta ātmani

TRANSLATION

The material modes—goodness, passion and ignorance—whose permutations are observed within a person's mind, are set into motion by the power of time.

PURPORT

The four ages described in these verses are manifestations of various modes of material nature. The age of truth, Satya-yuga, manifests the predominance of material goodness, and Kali-yuga manifests the predominance of ignorance. According to Śrīla Viśvanātha Cakravartī Ṭhākura, within each age the other three ages occasionally manifest as sub-ages. Thus even within Satya-yuga a demon in the mode of ignorance may appear, and within the age of Kali the highest religious principles may flourish for some time. As described in *Śrīmad-Bhāgavatam,* the three modes of nature are present everywhere and in everything, but the predominant mode, or combination of modes, determines the general character of any material phenomenon. In each age, therefore, the three modes are present in varying proportions. The particular age represented by goodness (Satya), passion (Tretā), passion and ignorance (Dvāpara) or ignorance (Kali) exists within each of the other ages as a subfactor.

TEXT 27

prabhavanti yadā sattve
mano-buddhīndriyāṇi ca
tadā kṛta-yugaṁ vidyāj
jñāne tapasi yad ruciḥ

TRANSLATION

When the mind, intelligence and senses are solidly fixed in the mode of goodness, that time should be understood as Satya-yuga, the age of truth. People then take pleasure in knowledge and austerity.

PURPORT

The word *kṛta* means "performed" or "executed." Thus in the age of truth all religious duties are duly performed, and people take great pleasure in spiritual knowledge and austerity. Even in the Kali-yuga, those who are situated in the mode of goodness take pleasure in the cultivation of spiritual knowledge and the regulated performance of austerity. This sublime state of existence is possible for one who has conquered sex desire.

TEXT 28

yadā karmasu kāmyeṣu
bhaktir yaśasi dehinām
tadā tretā rajo-vṛttir
iti jānīhi buddhiman

TRANSLATION

O most intelligent one, when the conditioned souls are devoted to their duties but have ulterior motives and seek personal prestige, you should understand such a situation to be the age of Tretā, in which the functions of passion are prominent.

TEXT 29

yadā lobhas tv asantoṣo
māno dambho 'tha matsaraḥ
karmaṇāṁ cāpi kāmyānāṁ
dvāparaṁ tad rajas-tamaḥ

TRANSLATION

When greed, dissatisfaction, false pride, hypocrisy and envy become prominent, along with attraction for selfish activities, such a time is the age of Dvāpara, dominated by the mixed modes of passion and ignorance.

TEXT 30

yadā māyānṛtaṁ tandrā
nidrā hiṁsā viṣādanam
śoka-mohau bhayaṁ dainyaṁ
sa kalis tāmasaḥ smṛtaḥ

TRANSLATION

When there is a predominance of cheating, lying, sloth, sleepiness, violence, depression, lamentation, bewilderment, fear and poverty, that age is Kali, the age of the mode of ignorance.

PURPORT

In Kali-yuga, people are almost exclusively devoted to gross materialism, with hardly any affinity for self-realization.

TEXT 31

tasmāt kṣudra-dṛśo martyāḥ
kṣudra-bhāgyā mahāśanāḥ
kāmino vitta-hīnāś ca
svairiṇyaś ca striyo 'satīḥ

TRANSLATION

Because of the bad qualities of the age of Kali, human beings will become shortsighted, unfortunate, gluttonous, lustful and poverty-stricken. The women, becoming unchaste, will freely wander from one man to the next.

PURPORT

In the age of Kali certain pseudointellectuals, seeking individual freedom, support sexual promiscuity. In fact, identification of the self with the body and the pursuit of "individual freedom" in the body rather than in the soul are signs of the most dismal ignorance and slavery to lust. When women are unchaste, many children are born out of wedlock as products of lust. These children grow up in psychologically unfavorable circumstances, and a neurotic, ignorant society arises. Symptoms of this are already manifest throughout the world.

TEXT 32

dasyūtkṛṣṭā janapadā
vedāḥ pāṣaṇḍa-dūṣitāḥ
rājānaś ca prajā-bhakṣāḥ
śiśnodara-parā dvijāḥ

TRANSLATION

Cities will be dominated by thieves, the *Vedas* will be contaminated by speculative interpretations of atheists, political leaders will virtually consume the citizens, and the so-called priests and intellectuals will be devotees of their bellies and genitals.

PURPORT

Many large cities are unsafe at night. For example, it is understood that no sane person will walk in New York's Central Park at night because he knows he will almost certainly be mugged. Apart from ordinary thieves, who abound in this age, large cities are filled with cutthroat businessmen, who enthusiastically convince people to purchase and consume useless or even harmful products. It has been well documented that beef, tobacco, liquor and many other modern products destroy one's physical health, what to speak of mental health, and yet modern capitalists do not hesitate to use every psychological trick in the book to convince people to consume these things. Modern cities are full of mental and atmospheric pollution, and even ordinary citizens are finding them unbearable.

This verse also points out that the teachings of the Vedic scriptures will be distorted in this age. Great universities teach courses on Hinduism in which Indian religion, despite limitless evidence to the contrary, is described as polytheistic and leading to an impersonal salvation. In fact, all Vedic literature is a unified whole, as stated by Lord Kṛṣṇa Himself in *Bhagavad-gītā* (15.15): *vedaiś ca sarvair aham eva vedyaḥ.* "By all the *Vedas* I [Kṛṣṇa] am to be known." All Vedic literature is meant for enlightening us about the Supreme Personal Absolute Truth—Viṣṇu, or Kṛṣṇa. Although known by many names and appearing in many forms, God is a single absolute entity, and He is a person. But this true Vedic understanding is hidden in the Kali-yuga.

In this verse Śukadeva astutely observes that "political leaders will virtually consume the citizens, and the so-called priests and intellectuals will be devotees of their bellies and genitals." How sadly true this statement is.

TEXT 33

avratā baṭavo 'śaucā
bhikṣavaś ca kuṭumbinaḥ
tapasvino grāma-vāsā
nyāsino 'tyartha-lolupāḥ

TRANSLATION

The *brahmacārīs* will fail to execute their vows and become generally unclean, the householders will become beggars, the *vānaprasthas* will live in the villages, and the *sannyāsīs* will become greedy for wealth.

PURPORT

Brahmacarya, celibate student life, is practically nonexistent in the age of Kali. In America, many boys' schools have become coeducational because young men frankly refuse to live without the constant companionship of lusty young girls. Also, we have personally observed throughout the Western world that student residences are among the dirtiest places on earth, as predicted here by the word *aśaucāḥ.*

Concerning householder beggars, when devotees of the Lord go door to door distributing transcendental literature and requesting donations for the propagation of God's glories, irritated householders commonly reply, "Someone should give *me* a donation." Householders in Kali-yuga are not charitable. Instead, because of their miserly mentality, they become irritated when spiritual mendicants approach them.

In Vedic culture, at the age of fifty, couples retire to sacred places for austere life and spiritual perfection. In countries like America, however, retirement cities have been constructed wherein elderly people can make fools of themselves by wasting the last years of their lives playing golf, ping-pong and shuffleboard and by engaging in pathetic attempts at love affairs even while their bodies are horribly rotting and their minds are growing senile. This shameless abuse of the venerable last years of life denotes a stubborn unwillingness to acknowledge the actual purpose of human life and is certainly an offense against God.

The words *nyāsino 'tyartha-lolupāḥ* indicate that charismatic religious leaders, and even those who are not charismatic, will proclaim themselves prophets, saints and incarnations to cheat the innocent public and fatten their bank accounts. Therefore the International Society for Krishna Consciousness is working arduously to establish bona fide celibate student life, religious householder life, dignified and progressive retirement, and genuine spiritual leadership for the entire world. Today, May 9, 1982, in the sensual city of Rio de Janeiro, Brazil, we have awarded *sannyāsa,* the renounced order of life, to three young men, two Brazilians and one American, with the sincere hope that they will faithfully execute the rigid vows of renounced life and provide authentic spiritual leadership in South America.

TEXT 34

hrasva-kāyā mahāhārā
bhūry-apatyā gata-hriyaḥ
śaśvat kaṭuka-bhāṣiṇyaś
caurya-māyoru-sāhasāḥ

TRANSLATION

Women will become much smaller in size, and they will eat too much, have more children than they can properly take care of, and lose all shyness. They will always speak harshly and will exhibit qualities of thievery, deceit and unrestrained audacity.

TEXT 35

paṇayiṣyanti vai kṣudrāḥ
kirāṭāḥ kūṭa-kāriṇaḥ
anāpady api maṁsyante
vārtāṁ sādhu jugupsitām

TRANSLATION

Businessmen will engage in petty commerce and earn their money by cheating. Even when there is no emergency, people will consider any degraded occupation quite acceptable.

PURPORT

Although other occupations are available, people do not hesitate to work in coal mines, slaughterhouses, steel mills, deserts, floating oil rigs, submarines and other equally abominable situations. As also mentioned here, businessmen will consider cheating and lying to be a perfectly respectable way to do business. These are all symptoms of the age of Kali.

TEXT 36

patiṁ tyakṣyanti nirdravyaṁ
bhṛtyā apy akhilottamam
bhṛtyaṁ vipannaṁ patayaḥ
kaulaṁ gāś cāpayasvinīḥ

TRANSLATION

Servants will abandon a master who has lost his wealth, even if that master is a saintly person of exemplary character. Masters will abandon an incapacitated servant, even if that servant has been in the family for generations. Cows will be abandoned or killed when they stop giving milk.

PURPORT

In India, the cow is considered sacred not because Indian people are primitive worshipers of mythological totems but because Hindus intelligently understand that the cow is a mother. As children, nearly all of us were nourished with cow's milk, and therefore the cow is one of our mothers. Certainly one's mother is sacred, and therefore we should not kill the sacred cow.

TEXT 37

pitṛ-bhrātṛ-suhṛj-jñātīn
hitvā saurata-sauhṛdāḥ
nanāndṛ-śyāla-saṁvādā
dīnāḥ straiṇāḥ kalau narāḥ

TRANSLATION

In Kali-yuga men will be wretched and controlled by women. They will reject their fathers, brothers, other relatives and friends and will instead associate with the sisters and brothers of their wives. Thus their conception of friendship will be based exclusively on sexual ties.

TEXT 38

śūdrāḥ pratigrahīṣyanti
tapo-veṣopajīvinaḥ
dharmaṁ vakṣyanty adharma-jñā
adhiruhyottamāsanam

TRANSLATION

Uncultured men will accept charity on behalf of the Lord and will earn their livelihood by making a show of austerity and wearing a mendicant's dress. Those who know nothing about religion will mount a high seat and presume to speak on religious principles.

PURPORT

The epidemic of bogus *gurus,* swamis, priests and so forth is explicitly described here.

TEXTS 39–40

nityam udvigna-manaso
durbhikṣa-kara-karśitāḥ
niranne bhū-tale rājan
anāvṛṣṭi-bhayāturāḥ
vāso-'nna-pāna-śayana-
vyavāya-snāna-bhūṣaṇaiḥ
hīnāḥ piśāca-sandarśā
bhaviṣyanti kalau prajāḥ

TRANSLATION

In the age of Kali, people's minds will always be agitated. They will become emaciated by famine and taxation, my dear King, and will always be disturbed by fear of drought. They will lack adequate clothing, food and drink, will be unable to properly rest, have sex or bathe themselves, and will have no ornaments to decorate their bodies. In fact, the people of Kali-yuga will gradually come to appear like ghostly, haunted creatures.

PURPORT

The symptoms described here are already prevalent in many countries of the world and will gradually spread to other places engulfed by impiety and materialism.

TEXT 41

kalau kākiṇike 'py arthe
vigṛhya tyakta-sauhṛdāḥ
tyakṣyanti ca priyān prāṇān
haniṣyanti svakān api

TRANSLATION

In Kali-yuga men will develop hatred for each other even over a few coins. Giving up all friendly relations, they will be ready to lose their own lives and kill even their own relatives.

TEXT 42

na rakṣiṣyanti manujāḥ
sthavirau pitarāv api
putrān bhāryāṁ ca kula-jāṁ
kṣudrāḥ śiśnodaraṁ-bharāḥ

TRANSLATION

Men will no longer protect their elderly parents, their children or their respectable wives. Thoroughly degraded, they will care only to satisfy their own bellies and genitals.

PURPORT

In this age many people are already sending their elderly parents away to lonely, and often bizarre, old-age homes, although the elderly parents spent their entire lives serving their children.

Young children are also tormented in many ways in this age. Suicide among children has increased dramatically in recent years because they are being born not to loving, religious parents but to degraded, selfish men and women. In fact, children are often born because a birth-control pill, a prophylactic or some other contraceptive device malfunctioned. Under such conditions, it is very difficult nowadays for parents to morally guide their children. Generally ignorant of spiritual science, parents cannot lead their children on the path of liberation and thus fail to fulfill their primary responsibility in family life.

As predicted in this verse, adultery has become common, and people in general are extremely concerned with eating and sex, which they consider far more important than knowing the Absolute Truth.

TEXT 43

kalau na rājan jagatāṁ paraṁ guruṁ
tri-loka-nāthānata-pāda-paṅkajam
prāyeṇa martyā bhagavantam acyutaṁ
yakṣyanti pāṣaṇḍa-vibhinna-cetasaḥ

TRANSLATION

O King, in the age of Kali people's intelligence will be diverted by atheism, and they will almost never offer sacrifice to the Supreme Personality of Godhead, who is the supreme spiritual master of the universe. Although the great personalities who control the three worlds all bow down to the lotus feet of the Supreme Lord, the petty and miserable human beings of this age will not do so.

PURPORT

The impulse to find the Absolute Truth, the source of all existence, has motivated philosophers, theologians and other intellectuals of various persuasions since time immemorial, and continues to do so today. However, soberly analyzing the ever-increasing plurality of so-called philosophies, religions, paths, ways of life and so on, we find that in almost all cases the ultimate objective is something impersonal or formless. But this idea of an impersonal or formless Absolute Truth has serious logical flaws. According to ordinary rules of logic, a particular effect should directly or indirectly embody the attributes, or nature, of its own cause. Thus that which has no personality or activity could hardly be the source of all personality and all activity.

Our irrepressible proclivity to philosophize about the ultimate truth often expresses itself through philosophical, scientific and mystical attempts to discover that from which everything emanates. This material world, which is a seemingly limitless network of interactive causes and effects, is certainly not the Absolute Truth, since scientific observation of material elements indicates that the stuff of this world, material energy, is endlessly transformed into different states and shapes. Therefore, one particular instance of material reality cannot be the ultimate source of all other things.

We may speculate that matter in some shape or other has always existed. This theory, however, is no longer attractive to modern cosmologists, such as those at the Massachusetts Institute of Technology. And even if we do posit that matter has always existed, we still must explain the source of consciousness if we want to satisfy our philosophical impulse toward discovering the Absolute Truth. Although modern empirical fanatics state that nothing is real except matter, everyone commonly experiences that consciousness is not the same kind of substance as a stone, a pencil or water. Awareness itself, in contradistinction to the objects of awareness, is not a physical entity but rather a process of perception and understanding. While there is ample evidence of a systematic interdependent relationship between matter and consciousness, there is no rigid empirical evidence whatsoever that matter is the *cause* of consciousness. Thus the theory that the material world has always existed and is therefore the ultimate truth does not scientifically or even intuitively explain the source of consciousness, which is the most fundamentally real aspect of our existence.

Furthermore, as demonstrated by Dr. Richard Thompson of the State University of New York at Binghamton and confirmed by several Nobel laureates in physics who have praised his work, the laws of nature governing the transformation of matter simply do not contain sufficiently complex information to account for the inconceivable complexity of events taking place within our own bodies and those of other life forms. In other words, not only do the material laws of nature fail to account for the existence of consciousness, but they cannot explain even the interaction of material elements at complex organic levels. Even Socrates, the first great Western philosopher, was disgusted with the attempt to establish ultimate causality in terms of mechanistic principles.

The heat and luminosity of the sun's rays demonstrate to the satisfaction of any rational man that the sun, the source of the rays, is certainly not a dark, cold globe but rather a reservoir of almost unlimited heat and light. Similarly, the innumerable instances of personality and personal consciousness within creation are more than adequate to demonstrate the existence, somewhere, of an unlimited reservoir of consciousness and personal behavior. In his dialogue *Philebus,* the Greek philosopher Plato argued that just as the material elements in our body are derived from a vast reservoir of material elements existing within the universe, our rational intelligence is also derived from a great cosmic intelligence existing within the universe, and this supreme intelligence is God, the creator. Unfortunately, in Kali-yuga many leading thinkers cannot understand this and instead deny that the Absolute Truth, the source of our personal consciousness, has consciousness and personality. This is as reasonable as saying that the sun is cold and dark.

In Kali-yuga, many people present cheap, stereotyped arguments, such as "If God had a body or personality, He would be limited." In this inadequate attempt at logic, a qualified term is falsely presented in a universal sense. What really should be said is, "If God had a *material* body or a *material* personality like those we have experienced, He would be limited." But we leave out the qualifying adjective *material* and make a pseudouniversal assertion, as if we understood the full range, within total reality, of bodies and personality.

Bhagavad-gītā, Śrīmad-Bhāgavatam and other Vedic literatures teach that the transcendental form and personality of the Absolute Truth are unlimited. Clearly, to be truly infinite God must be not only quantitatively but also qualitatively infinite. Unfortunately, in our mechanistic, industrial age we tend to define infinity only in its quantitative sense, and thus we fail to notice that an infinity of personal qualities is a necessary aspect of infinity. In other words, God must have infinite beauty, infinite wealth, infinite intelligence, infinite humor, infinite kindness, infinite anger and so on. Infinite is an absolute, and if anything we observe in this world is not contained, somehow or other, within our conception of the Absolute, then that conception is of something limited and not of the Absolute at all.

Only in Kali-yuga are there philosophers foolish enough to proudly define the most absolute of all terms—God—in materialistic, relative ways and then declare themselves enlightened thinkers. No matter how big our brain may be, we should have the common sense to place it at the feet of the Supreme Personality of Godhead.

TEXT 44

yan-nāmadheyaṁ mriyamāṇa āturaḥ
patan skhalan vā vivaśo gṛṇan pumān
vimukta-karmārgala uttamāṁ gatiṁ
prāpnoti yakṣyanti na taṁ kalau janāḥ

TRANSLATION

Terrified, about to die, a man collapses on his bed. Although his voice is faltering and he is hardly conscious of what he is saying, if he utters the holy name of the Supreme Lord he can be freed from the reaction of his fruitive work and achieve the supreme destination. But still people in the age of Kali will not worship the Supreme Lord.

PURPORT

You can lead a horse to water, but you cannot make him drink.

TEXT 45

puṁsāṁ kali-kṛtān doṣān
dravya-deśātma-sambhavān
sarvān harati citta-stho
bhagavān puruṣottamaḥ

TRANSLATION

In the Kali-yuga, objects, places and even individual personalities are all polluted. The almighty Personality of Godhead, however, can remove all such contamination from the life of one who fixes the Lord within his mind.

TEXT 46

śrutaḥ saṅkīrtito dhyātaḥ
pūjitaś cādṛto 'pi vā
nṛṇāṁ dhunoti bhagavān
hṛt-stho janmāyutāśubham

TRANSLATION

If a person hears about, glorifies, meditates upon, worships or simply offers great respect to the Supreme Lord, who is situated within the heart, the Lord will remove from his mind the contamination accumulated during many thousands of lifetimes.

TEXT 47

yathā hemni sthito vahnir
durvarṇaṁ hanti dhātu-jam
evam ātma-gato viṣṇur
yoginām aśubhāśayam

TRANSLATION

Just as fire applied to gold removes any discoloration caused by traces of other metals, Lord Viṣṇu within the heart purifies the minds of the *yogīs.*

PURPORT

Although one may practice the mystic *yoga* system, his actual spiritual advancement is due to the mercy of the Supreme Lord within the heart; it is not directly the result of his austerity and meditation. If one becomes foolishly proud in the name of *yoga,* his spiritual position becomes ridiculous.

TEXT 48

vidyā-tapaḥ-prāṇa-nirodha-maitrī-
tīrthābhiṣeka-vrata-dāna-japyaiḥ
nātyanta-śuddhiṁ labhate 'ntarātmā
yathā hṛdi-sthe bhagavaty anante

TRANSLATION

By one's engaging in the processes of demigod worship, austerities, breath control, compassion, bathing in holy places, strict vows, charity and chanting of various *mantras*, one's mind cannot attain the same absolute purification as that achieved when the unlimited Personality of Godhead appears within one's heart.

TEXT 49

tasmāt sarvātmanā rājan
hṛdi-sthaṁ kuru keśavam
mriyamāṇo hy avahitas
tato yāsi parāṁ gatim

TRANSLATION

Therefore, O King, endeavor with all your might to fix the Supreme Lord Keśava within your heart. Maintain this concentration upon the Lord, and at the time of death you will certainly attain the supreme destination.

PURPORT

Although the Supreme Lord is always in the heart of every living being, the words *hṛdi-sthaṁ kuru keśavam* indicate that one should endeavor to realize the Lord's presence there and maintain this awareness at every moment. Parīkṣit Mahārāja is about to give up this world and is receiving final instructions from his spiritual master, Śukadeva Gosvāmī. In the context of the King's imminent departure, this verse has special significance.

TEXT 50

mriyamāṇair abhidhyeyo
bhagavān parameśvaraḥ
ātma-bhāvaṁ nayaty aṅga
sarvātmā sarva-saṁśrayaḥ

TRANSLATION

My dear King, the Personality of Godhead is the ultimate controller. He is the Supreme Soul and the supreme shelter of all beings. When meditated upon by those about to die, He reveals to them their own eternal spiritual identity.

TEXT 51

kaler doṣa-nidhe rājann
asti hy eko mahān guṇaḥ
kīrtanād eva kṛṣṇasya
mukta-saṅgaḥ paraṁ vrajet

TRANSLATION

My dear King, although Kali-yuga is an ocean of faults, there is still one good quality about this age: Simply by chanting the Hare Kṛṣṇa *mahā-mantra*, one can become free from material bondage and be promoted to the transcendental kingdom.

PURPORT

After mentioning the innumerable faults of this age of Kali, Śukadeva Gosvāmī now mentions its one brilliant aspect. Just as one powerful king can kill innumerable thieves, one brilliant spiritual quality can destroy all the contamination of this age. It is impossible to overestimate the importance of chanting Hare Kṛṣṇa, Hare Kṛṣṇa, Kṛṣṇa Kṛṣṇa, Hare Hare/ Hare Rāma, Hare Rāma, Rāma Rāma, Hare Hare, especially in this fallen age.

TEXT 52

kṛte yad dhyāyato viṣṇuṁ
tretāyāṁ yajato makhaiḥ
dvāpare paricaryāyāṁ
kalau tad dhari-kīrtanāt

TRANSLATION

Whatever result was obtained in Satya-yuga by meditating on Viṣṇu, in Tretā-yuga by performing sacrifices, and in Dvāpara-yuga by serving the Lord's lotus feet can be obtained in Kali-yuga simply by chanting the Hare Kṛṣṇa *mahā-mantra.*

PURPORT

A similar verse is found in the *Viṣṇu Purāṇa* (6.2.17), and also in the *Padma Purāṇa* (*Uttara-khaṇḍa* 72.25) and the *Bṛhan-nāradiya Purāṇa* (38.97):

dhyāyan kṛte yajan yajñais
tretāyāṁ dvāpare 'rcayan
yad āpnoti tad āpnoti
kalau saṅkīrtya keśavam

"Whatever is achieved by meditation in Satya-yuga, by the performance of sacrifice in Tretā-yuga, and by the worship of Lord Kṛṣṇa's lotus feet in Dvāpara-yuga is obtained in the age of Kali simply by glorifying the name of Lord Keśava."

Śrīla Jīva Gosvāmī has further quoted from the *Brahma-vaivarta Purāṇa* concerning the degraded condition of people in Kali-yuga:

ataḥ kalau tapo-yoga-
vidyā-yajñādikāḥ kriyāḥ
sāṅgā bhavanti na kṛtāḥ
kuśalair api dehibhiḥ

"Thus in the age of Kali the practices of austerity, *yoga* meditation, Deity worship, sacrifice and so on, along with their various subsidiary functions, are not properly carried out, even by the most expert embodied souls."

Śrīla Jīva Gosvāmī has also cited the *Cātur-māsya-māhātmya* of the *Skanda Purāṇa* concerning the necessity of chanting Hare Kṛṣṇa in this age:

tathā caivottamaṁ loke
tapaḥ śrī-hari-kīrtanam
kalau yuge viśeṣeṇa
viṣṇu-prītyai samācaret

"In this way the most perfect penance to be executed in this world is the chanting of the name of Lord Śrī Hari. Especially in the age of Kali, one can satisfy the Supreme Lord Viṣṇu by performing *saṅkīrtana*."

In conclusion, massive propaganda should be made all over the world to induce people to chant the Hare Kṛṣṇa *mantra*, by which human society can be rescued from the dangerous ocean of the age of Kali.

Section II

Material Problems, Spiritual Solutions

A fish that is taken out of water cannot be happy by any arrangement on land. He must be supplied with water. In the same way, the minute *sac-cid-ānanda* living entity cannot be really happy through any amount of planning conceived by his illusioned brain in this material universe. He must therefore be given a different type of happiness which is spiritual in essence. Our ambition should be aimed at enjoying spiritual bliss and not this temporary happiness. Some philosophers claim that spiritual bliss is attained by negating material happiness and material existence. Theoretical negation of material activities as propounded by Śrīpāda Śaṅkarācārya may be effective for an insignificant section of mankind, but the best and surest way for everyone to attain spiritual bliss was propounded by Lord Śrī Caitanya Mahāprabhu by means of devotional activities. These devotional activities can change the very face of material nature.

Śrīmad-Bhāgavatam tells about the secret of attaining complete satisfaction:

sa vai puṁsāṁ paro dharmo
yato bhaktir adhokṣaje
ahaituky apratihatā
yayātmā suprasīdati

(Śrīmad-Bhāgavatam 1.2.6)

TRANSLATION

The supreme occupation [dharma] for all humanity is that by which men can attain to loving devotional service unto the transcendent Lord. Such devotional service must be unmotivated and uninterrupted to completely satisfy the self.

PURPORT

In this statement, Śrī Sūta Gosvāmī answers the first question of the sages of Naimiṣāraṇya. The sages asked him to summarize the whole range of revealed scriptures and present the most essential part so that fallen people or the people in general might easily take it up. The *Vedas* prescribe two different types of occupation for the human being. One is called the *pravṛtti-mārga,* or the path of sense enjoyment, and the other is called the *nivṛtti-mārga*, or the path of renunciation. The path of enjoyment is inferior, and the path of sacrifice for the supreme cause is superior. The material existence of the living being is a diseased condition of actual life. Actual life is spiritual existence, or *brahma-bhūta* existence, where life is eternal, blissful and full of knowledge. Material existence is temporary, illusory and full of miseries. There is no happiness at all. There is just the futile attempt to get rid of the miseries, and temporary cessation of misery is falsely called happiness. Therefore, the path of progressive material enjoyment, which is temporary, miserable and illusory, is inferior. But devotional service to the Supreme Lord, which leads one to eternal, blissful and all-cognizant life, is called the superior quality of occupation. This is sometimes polluted when mixed with the inferior quality. For example, adoption of devotional service for material gain is certainly an obstruction to the progressive path of renunciation. Renunciation or abnegation for ultimate good is certainly a better occupation than enjoyment in the diseased condition of life. Such enjoyment only aggravates the symptoms of disease and increases its duration. Therefore devotional service to the Lord must be pure in quality, i.e., without the least desire for material enjoyment. One should, therefore, accept the superior quality of occupation in the form of the devotional service of the Lord without any tinge of unnecessary desire, fruitive action and philosophical speculation. This alone can lead one to perpetual solace in His service.

We have purposely denoted *dharma* as occupation because the root meaning of the word *dharma* is "that which sustains one's existence." A living being's sustenance of existence is to coordinate his activities with his eternal relation with the Supreme Lord Kṛṣṇa. Kṛṣṇa is the central pivot of living beings, and He is the all-attractive living entity or eternal form amongst all other living beings or eternal forms. Each and every living being has his eternal form in the spiritual existence, and Kṛṣṇa is the eternal attraction for all of them. Kṛṣṇa is the complete whole, and everything else is His part and parcel. The relation is one of the servant and the served. It is transcendental and is completely distinct from our experience in material existence. This relation of servant and the served is the most congenial form of intimacy. One can realize it as devotional service progresses. Everyone should engage himself in that transcendental loving service of the Lord, even in the present conditional state of material existence. That will gradually give one the clue to actual life and please him to complete satisfaction.

CHAPTER 3

Solving the Real Problems

Knowing the Real Problems

In the *Bhagavad-gītā* it is said that one who is intelligent, he will see four things before him. You may be very great scientist. You may be very much advanced in material science. You may be able to construct very high building, skyscrapers, and many millions of motorcars, but you have to think whether you have solved the real problem of life. *The real problem of life is birth, death, disease, and old age.* Not that to live in a high skyscraper our problems of life is solved. No. The problem of life is how to stop these four things: birth, death, old age, and disease. But we have neglected the real problems of life. And we are misusing our intelligence for constructing big buildings and constructing or increasing the so-called bodily necessities of life. The bodily necessities of life are four only. What is that? Eating, sleeping, mating, and defending. To maintain this body you require to eat something. Everyone is eating. You are eating, the cats are eating, the dogs are eating, the birds are eating. They have no economic problem. Eating is there already. Have you seen ever that a bird is dying for want of eating, eatables? No. So these things are already arranged. That is no problem. In every form of life your eatables are there by nature's supply. Similarly sleeping. The bird is sleeping, the dog is sleeping, the cat is sleeping, and you are also sleeping. But you have got a very nice apartment. Does it mean that you have solved the problem of sleeping? No. Then defending. The birds, the dogs, the cats, the animals, everyone knows how to defend in their own way. You go every day in the, what is called, Stowe Lake path. And as soon as you go, the swans immediately jump to the water because that is their defending. As soon as they go to the water, they know that "These human beings, they cannot come to the water. We are now secure." So that defending process is there even in the swans, in the birds, in everything. You don't think that because we have manufactured atomic bombs, therefore we have become very good. What is this atomic bomb? Killing. Killing is going on. Have you manufactured anything by which you can save from death?

Suffering—from Womb to Tomb

This material world is called *samsrti,* continuously suffering. That we cannot understand. This is called ignorance. Continuously suffering. They are thinking, "We are very happy," but this material world means continuously suffering. So when a living entity dies, his gross body is left behind and the subtle body—mind, intelligence & ego—carries him in another body through the semina of the father to the womb of the mother. In the womb, the body again forms, and when the body is formed, then he comes out from the womb. And within the womb of the mother there is so much suffering, we know that. Many times we have discussed. And coming, from the very moment the child is crying, there are inconveniences. So many things are there which he cannot express. In this way, within the womb there is suffering, out of the womb there is suffering. Then growing, child or baby or boy, there are so many sufferings. Then young man—suppose he becomes family man—then earn for the family. That is also suffering. Then old man, disease, inability, many, many thoughts, that is also suffering. And again death is suffering.

The following verses from the *Śrīmad-Bhāgavatam* tell about the agonizing experience of the fetus in the womb:

kṛmibhiḥ kṣata-sarvāṅgaḥ
saukumāryāt pratikṣaṇam
mūrcchām āpnoty uru-kleśas
tatratyaiḥ kṣudhitair muhuḥ

(Śrīmad-Bhāgavatam 3.31.6)

TRANSLATION

Bitten again and again all over the body by the hungry worms in the abdomen itself, the child suffers terrible agony because of his tenderness. He thus becomes unconscious moment after moment because of the terrible condition.

PURPORT

The miserable condition of material existence is not only felt when we come out of the womb of the mother, but is also present within the womb. Miserable life begins from the moment the living entity begins to contact his material body. Unfortunately, we forget this experience and do not take the miseries of birth very seriously. In *Bhagavad-gītā*, therefore, it is specifically mentioned that one should be very alert to understand the specific difficulties of birth and death. Just as during the formation of this body we have to pass through so many difficulties within the womb of the mother, at the time of death there are also many difficulties. As described in the previous chapter, one has to transmigrate from one body to another, and the transmigration into the bodies of dogs and hogs is especially miserable. But despite such miserable conditions, due to the spell of māyā we forget everything and become enamored by the present so-called happiness, which is described as actually no more than a counteraction to distress.

kaṭu-tīkṣṇoṣṇa-lavaṇa-
rūkṣāmlādibhir ulbaṇaiḥ
mātṛ-bhuktair upaspṛṣṭaḥ
sarvāṅgotthita-vedanaḥ

(*Śrīmad-Bhāgavatam* 3.31.7)

TRANSLATION

Owing to the mother's eating bitter, pungent foodstuffs, or food which is too salty or too sour, the body of the child incessantly suffers pains which are almost intolerable.

PURPORT

All descriptions of the child's bodily situation in the womb of the mother are beyond our conception. It is very difficult to remain in such a position, but still the child has to remain. Because his consciousness is not very developed, the child can tolerate it, otherwise he would die. That is the benediction of *māyā,* who endows the suffering body with the qualifications for tolerating such terrible tortures.

ulbena saṁvṛtas tasminn
antraiś ca bahir āvṛtaḥ
āste kṛtvā śiraḥ kukṣau
bhugna-pṛṣṭha-śirodharaḥ

(*Śrīmad-Bhāgavatam* 3.31.8)

TRANSLATION

Placed within the amnion and covered outside by the intestines, the child remains lying on one side of the abdomen, his head turned towards his belly and his back and neck arched like a bow.

PURPORT

If a grown man were put into such a condition as the child within the abdomen, completely entangled in all respects, it would be impossible for him to live even for a few seconds. Unfortunately, we forget all these sufferings and try to be happy in this life, not caring for the liberation of the soul from the entanglement of birth and death. It is an unfortunate civilization in which these matters are not plainly discussed to make people understand the precarious condition of material existence.

akalpaḥ svāṅga-ceṣṭāyāṁ
śakunta iva pañjare
tatra labdha-smṛtir daivāt
karma janma-śatodbhavam
smaran dīrgham anucchvāsaṁ
śarma kiṁ nāma vindate

(Śrīmad-Bhāgavatam 3.31.9)

TRANSLATION

The child thus remains just like a bird in a cage, without freedom of movement. At that time, if the child is fortunate, he can remember all the troubles of his past one hundred births, and he grieves wretchedly. What is the possibility of peace of mind in that condition?

PURPORT

After birth the child may forget about the difficulties of his past lives, but when we are grown-up we can at least understand the grievous tortures undergone at birth and death by reading the authorized scriptures like *Śrīmad-Bhāgavatam.* If we do not believe in the scriptures, that is a different question, but if we have faith in the authority of such descriptions, then we must prepare for our freedom in the next life; that is possible in this human form of life. One who does not take heed of these indications of suffering in human existence is said to be undoubtedly committing suicide. It is said that this human form of life is the only means for crossing over the nescience of *māyā*, or material existence. We have a very efficient boat in this human form of body, and there is a very expert captain, the spiritual master; the scriptural injunctions are like favorable winds. If we do not cross over the ocean of the nescience of material existence in spite of all these facilities, then certainly we are all intentionally committing suicide.

The miseries experienced on coming out of the womb are explained as follows:

tenāvasṛṣṭaḥ sahasā
kṛtvāvāk śira āturaḥ
viniṣkrāmati kṛcchreṇa
nirucchvāso hata-smṛtiḥ

(Śrīmad-Bhāgavatam 3.31.23)

TRANSLATION

Pushed downward all of a sudden by the wind, the child comes out with great trouble, head downward, breathless and deprived of memory due to severe agony.

PURPORT

The word *kṛcchreṇa* means "with great difficulty." When the child comes out of the abdomen through the narrow passage, due to pressure there the breathing system completely stops, and due to agony the child loses his memory. Sometimes the trouble is so severe that the child comes out dead or almost dead. One can imagine what the pangs of birth are like. The child remains for ten months in that horrible condition within the abdomen, and at the end of ten months he is forcibly pushed out. In *Bhagavad-gītā* the Lord points out that a person who is serious about advancement in spiritual consciousness should always consider the four pangs of birth, death, disease and old age. The materialist advances in many ways, but he is unable to stop these four principles of suffering inherent in material existence.

patito bhuvy asṛṅ-miśraḥ
viṣṭhā-bhūr iva ceṣṭate
rorūyati gate jñāne
viparītāṁ gatiṁ gataḥ

(Śrīmad-Bhāgavatam 3.31.24)

TRANSLATION

The child thus falls on the ground, smeared with stool and blood, and plays just like a worm germinated from the stool. He loses his superior knowledge and cries under the spell of *māyā*.

para-cchandaṁ na viduṣā
puṣyamāṇo janena saḥ
anabhipretam āpannaḥ
pratyākhyātum anīśvaraḥ

(Śrīmad-Bhāgavatam 3.31.25)

TRANSLATION

After coming out of the abdomen, the child is given to the care of persons who are unable to understand what he wants, and thus he is nursed by such persons. Unable to refuse whatever is given to him, he falls into undesirable circumstances.

PURPORT

Within the abdomen of the mother, the nourishment of the child was being carried on by nature's own arrangement. The atmosphere within the abdomen was not at all pleasing, but as far as the child's feeding was concerned, it was being properly done by the laws of nature. But upon coming out of the abdomen the child falls into a different atmosphere. He wants to eat one thing, but something else is given to him because no one knows his actual demand, and he cannot refuse the undesirables given to him. Sometimes the child cries for the mother's breast, but because the nurse thinks that it is due to pain within his stomach that he is crying, she supplies him some bitter medicine. The child does not want it, but he cannot refuse it. He is put in very awkward circumstances, and the suffering continues.

śāyito 'śuci-paryaṅke
jantuḥ svedaja-dūṣite
neśaḥ kaṇḍūyane 'ṅgānām
āsanotthāna-ceṣṭane

(Śrīmad-Bhāgavatam 3.31.26)

TRANSLATION

Laid down on a foul bed infested with sweat and germs, the poor child is incapable of scratching his body to get relief from his itching sensation to say nothing of sitting up, standing or even moving.

PURPORT

It should be noted that the child is born crying and suffering. After birth the same suffering continues, and he cries. Because he is disturbed by the germs in his foul bed, which is contaminated by his urine and stool, the poor child continues to cry. He is unable to take any remedial measure for his relief.

tudanty āma-tvacaṁ daṁśā
maśakā matkuṇādayaḥ
rudantaṁ vigata-jñānaṁ
kṛmayaḥ kṛmikaṁ yathā

(*Śrīmad-Bhāgavatam* 3.31.27)

TRANSLATION

In his helpless condition, gnats, mosquitoes, bugs and other germs bite the baby, whose skin is tender, just as smaller worms bite a big worm. The child, deprived of his wisdom, cries bitterly.

PURPORT

The word *vigata jñānam* means that the spiritual knowledge which the child developed in the abdomen is already lost to the spell of *māyā*. Owing to various kinds of disturbances and to being out of the abdomen, the child cannot remember what he was thinking of for his salvation. It is assumed that even if a person acquires some spiritually uplifting knowledge, circumstantially he is prone to forget it. Not only children but also elderly persons should be very careful to protect their sense of Kṛṣṇa consciousness and avoid unfavorable circumstances so that they may not forget their prime duty.

ity evaṁ śaiśavaṁ bhuktvā
duḥkhaṁ paugaṇḍam eva ca
alabdhābhīpsito 'jñānād
iddha-manyuḥ śucārpitaḥ

(*Śrīmad-Bhāgavatam* 3.31.28)

TRANSLATION

In this way, the child passes through his childhood, suffering different kinds of distress, and attains boyhood. In boyhood also he suffers pain over desires to get things he can never achieve. And thus, due to ignorance, he becomes angry and sorry.

PURPORT

From birth to the end of five years of age is called childhood. After five years up to the end of the fifteenth year is called *paugaṇḍa.* At sixteen years of age, youth begins. The distresses of childhood are already explained, but when the child attains boyhood he is enrolled in a school which he does not like. He wants to play, but he is forced to go to school and study and take responsibility for passing examinations. Another kind of distress is that he wants to get some things with which to play, but circumstances may be such that he is not able to attain them, and he thus becomes aggrieved and feels pain. In one word, he is unhappy, even in his boyhood, just as he was unhappy in his childhood, what to speak of youth. Boys are apt to create so many artificial demands for playing, and when they do not attain satisfaction they become furious with anger, and the result is suffering.

saha dehena mānena
vardhamānena manyunā
karoti vigrahaṁ kāmī
kāmiṣv antāya cātmanaḥ

(Śrīmad-Bhāgavatam 3.31.29)

TRANSLATION

With the growth of the body, the living entity, in order to vanquish his soul, increases his false prestige and anger and thereby creates enmity towards similarly lusty people.

PURPORT

In *Bhagavad-gītā*, Third Chapter, verse 36, Arjuna inquired from Kṛṣṇa about the cause of a living being's lust. It is said that a living entity is eternal and, as such, qualitatively one with the Supreme Lord. Then what is the reason he falls prey to the material and commits so many sinful activities by the influence of the material energy? In reply to this question, Lord Kṛṣṇa said that it is lust which causes a living entity to glide down from his exalted position to the abominable condition of material existence. This lust circumstantially changes into anger. Both lust and anger stand on the platform of the mode of passion. Lust is actually the product of the mode of passion, and in the absence of satisfaction of lust, the same desire transforms into anger on the platform of ignorance. When ignorance covers the soul, it is the source of his degradation to the most abominable condition of hellish life.

To raise oneself from hellish life to the highest position of spiritual understanding is to transform this lust into love of Kṛṣṇa. Śrī Narottama dāsa Ṭhākura, a great *ācārya* of the Vaiṣṇava *sampradāya*, said, kāma *kṛṣṇa-karmārpaṇe:* due to our lust, we want many things for our sense gratification, but the same lust can be transformed in a purified way so that we want everything for the satisfaction of the Supreme Personality of Godhead. Anger also can be utilized towards a person who is atheistic or who is envious of the Personality of Godhead. As we have fallen into this material existence because of our lust and anger, the same two qualities can be utilized for the purpose of advancing in Kṛṣṇa consciousness, and one can elevate himself again to his former pure, spiritual position. Śrīla Rūpa Gosvāmī has therefore recommended that because in material existence we have so many objects of sense gratification, which we need for the maintenance of the body, we should use all of them without attachment, for the purpose of satisfying the senses of Kṛṣṇa; that is actual renunciation.

The process of suffering here in this material world is represented by *'pa-varga'*. Different stages of suffering is called *pavarga*. The first thing is *pa*. This is *pa pha ba bha ma, pa-varga*. There are five *vargas* in Sanskrit grammar: *ka-varga*, *ca-varga*, *ta-varga*, *ta-varga*, and *pa-varga*. Those who know, I mean to say, Sanskrit grammar, they will understand. So *pa-varga* means these five alphabets, *pa pha ba bha ma*. So our sufferings... First of all, labor, *parisrama*. *Pa*. You cannot get anything in this material world without laboring. That is not possible. Just like we have got this nice temple. How we have got it? Laboring. We have to collect the stone, we have to collect this brick, we have to... If I cannot work personally, then I have to engage laborer. So this temple is not by accident, automatically, by chunk it has come. No. There must be labor. *Parisrama*. That is *pa*. Then *pha*. *Pha*, in the English you can say frustration. Or in Sanskrit the *phena*, and English word is foam. When you work very hard, everyone, you know, there is foam. We have generally seen, in animals there is foam, in horse. The, hard labor, very hard labor, the foam comes. So first of all, *parisrama*, hard labor, then foam. *Pa pha*. And *ba*. *Ba* means *vyarthata*. Frustration. Despite so much hard labor, still frustration. Now our leaders are advertising that "Work hard. Work hard." "Sir, I am working so hard that I am working like an ass, like an animal, and I am tired. Still I have to work hard?" "Yes." This is samsrti.

So this is called *vyarthata*. You work hard, hard, hard. Still you'll not be successful. You'll have to work hard. That is called *pa*, *pha*, *ba*. And *bha*, *bha* means fearfulness. Just like the animal is working so hard and still he's afraid. "The master may whip." "You are not working?" Phut! Phut! He has to work still. Bhaya. So that fearfulness is everywhere. *Ahara-nidra-bhaya-maithunam ca samanyam etat pasubhir naranam*. The ox and bull, they are afraid of the driver, and we are afraid of our leader, of our government, of our so-called master and so on, so on, so on. That you cannot avoid. That is not possible. *Sada samudvigna-dhiyam asad-grahat*. Because we have accepted this material body, we have to be always remain in anxiety. You cannot avoid. So *pa*, *pha*, *ba*, *bha*, and at last, *ma*. *Ma* means *mrtyu* or death. And again *pa*, again begin with *pa*. This is going on. This is called Repeatedly, *pa*, *pha*, *ba*, *bha*, *ma*; *pa*, *pha*, *ba*,*bha*, *ma*. So if you take to Krsna consciousness, then this *pavarga—pa*, *pha*, *ba*, *bha*, *ma*—will be counteracted. Not otherwise. Not otherwise. It is not possible.

Ultimately, anyone who has taken birth in this world has to surrender everything very dear to him including one's life:

ena caivābhipanno 'yaṁ
prāṇaiḥ priyatamair api
janaḥ sadyo viyujyeta
kim utānyair dhanādibhiḥ

(Śrīmad-Bhāgavatam 1.13.20)

TRANSLATION

Whoever is under the influence of supreme kāla [eternal time] must surrender his most dear life, and what to speak of other things, such as wealth, honor, children, land and home.

PURPORT

A great Indian scientist, busy in the planmaking business, was suddenly called by invincible eternal time while going to attend a very important meeting of the planning commission, and he had to surrender his life, wife, children, house, land, wealth, etc. During the political upsurge in India and its division into Pakistan and Hindustan, so many rich and influential Indians had to surrender life, property and honor due to the influence of time, and there are hundreds and thousands of examples like that all over the world, all over the universe, which are all effects of the influence of time. Therefore, the conclusion is that there is no powerful living being within the universe who can overcome the influence of time. Many poets have written verses lamenting the influence of time. Many devastations have taken place over the universes due to the influence of time, and no one could check them by any means. Even in our daily life, so many things come and go in which we have no hand, but we have to suffer or tolerate them without remedial measure. That is the result of time.

The Special Prerogative of Human Life

The *Bhagavad-gītā* says that out of many thousands of human beings, one may try to make perfection of his life. Man is an animal, but he has one special prerogative, rational thought. What is that rational thought? Reasoning power, argument. Now, reasoning power is there in dogs and cats as well. Suppose a dog comes up to you; if you say, "Hut!" he'll understand. The dog will understand that you don't want him. So, he has some reasoning power. But what is the special reasoning power of the human being?

As far as the bodily necessities are concerned, the reasoning power is there even in the animal. If a cat wants to steal some milk from your kitchen, she has very nice reasoning power: she is always looking to see when the master is out and she can take. So, for the four propensities of animal life—eating, sleeping, mating and defending—there is reasoning power even in beasts. Then, what is the special reasoning power of the human being, by which he is called the rational animal?

The special reasoning power is to inquire, "Why am I suffering?" This is special reasoning. The animals are suffering, but they do not know how to remedy the suffering. But human beings are making scientific advancement and philosophical advancement, cultural advancement, religious advancement—progress in so many lines—because they want to be happy. "Where is the point of happiness?" This reasoning power is especially given to the human being. Therefore, in the *Bhagavad-gītā*, Kṛṣṇa says, "Out of so many men, one may know Me."

Generally, the people are just like animals. They simply do not know anything beyond the necessities of the body: how to eat, how to sleep, how to mate and how to defend. And the *Bhagavad-gītā* says, out of many thousands, someone may develop this reasoning power: "Why am I suffering?" He asks this question: "Why am I suffering?" We do not want to suffer, but suffering is forced upon us. We do not want too much cold, but too much cold and too much heat are forced upon us.

When there is some impetus to awaken this reasoning power, it is called *brahma jijñāsā*. This is found in the *Vedānta-sūtra*. The first verse says that now, this human form of life is meant for asking the question of how to solve the problem of suffering.

The vedic literatues are composed specifically to solve the problem of suffering:

anarthopaśamaṁ sākṣād
bhakti-yogam adhokṣaje
lokasyājānato vidvāṁś
cakre sātvata-saṁhitām

(*Śrīmad-Bhāgavatam 1.7.6*)

TRANSLATION

The material miseries of the living entity, which are superfluous to him, can be directly mitigated by the linking process of devotional service. But the mass of people do not know this, and therefore the learned Vyāsadeva compiled this Vedic literature, which is in relation to the Supreme Truth.

PURPORT

Śrīla Vyāsadeva saw the all-perfect Personality of Godhead. This statement suggests that the complete unit of the Personality of Godhead includes His parts and parcels also. He saw, therefore, His different energies, namely the internal energy, the marginal energy and the external energy. He also saw His different plenary portions and parts of the plenary portions, namely His different incarnations also, and he specifically observed the unwanted miseries of the conditioned souls, who are bewildered by the external energy. And at last he saw the remedial measure for the conditioned souls, namely, the process of devotional service. It is a great transcendental science and begins with the process of hearing and chanting the name, fame, glory, etc., of the Supreme Personality of Godhead. Revival of the dormant affection or love of Godhead does not depend on the mechanical system of hearing and chanting, but it solely and wholly depends on the causeless mercy of the Lord. When the Lord is fully satisfied with the sincere efforts of the devotee, He may endow him with His loving transcendental service. But even with the prescribed forms of hearing and chanting, there is at once mitigation of the superfluous and unwanted miseries of material existence. Such mitigation of material affection does not wait for development of transcendental knowledge. Rather, knowledge is dependent on devotional service for the ultimate realization of the Supreme Truth.

yasyāṁ vai śrūyamāṇāyāṁ
kṛṣṇe parama-pūruṣe
bhaktir utpadyate puṁsaḥ
śoka-moha-bhayāpahā

(Śrīmad-Bhāgavatam 1.7.7)

TRANSLATION

Simply by giving aural reception to this Vedic literature, the feeling for loving devotional service to Lord Kṛṣṇa, the Supreme Personality of Godhead, sprouts up at once to extinguish the fire of lamentation, illusion and fearfulness.

PURPORT

There are various senses, of which the ear is the most effective. This sense works even when a man is deep asleep. One can protect himself from the hands of an enemy while awake, but while asleep one is protected by the ear only. The importance of hearing is mentioned here in connection with attaining the highest perfection of life, namely, getting free from three material pangs. Everyone is full of lamentation at every moment, he is after the mirage of illusory things, and he is always afraid of his supposed enemy. These are the primary symptoms of material disease. And it is definitely suggested herein that simply by hearing the message of *Śrīmad-Bhāgavatam* one gets attachment for the Supreme Personality of Godhead Śrī Kṛṣṇa, and as soon as this is effected the symptoms of the material diseases disappear. Śrīla Vyāsadeva saw the all-perfect Personality of Godhead, and in this statement the all-perfect Personality of Godhead Śrī Kṛṣṇa is clearly confirmed.

The ultimate result of devotional service is to develop genuine love for the Supreme Personality. Love is a word which is often used in relation with man and woman. And love is the only word that can be properly used to indicate the relation between Lord Kṛṣṇa and the living entities. The living entities are mentioned as *prakṛti* in the *Bhagavad-gītā*, and in Sanskrit *prakṛti* is a feminine object. The Lord is always described as the *parama-puruṣa*, or the supreme male personality. Thus the affection between the Lord and the living entities is something like that between the male and the female. Therefore the term love of Godhead is quite appropriate.

Loving devotional service to the Lord begins with hearing about the Lord. There is no difference between the Lord and the subject matter heard about Him. The Lord is absolute in all respects, and thus there is no difference between Him and the subject matter heard about Him. Therefore, hearing about Him means immediate contact with Him by the process of vibration of the transcendental sound. And the transcendental sound is so effective that it acts at once by removing all material affections mentioned above. As mentioned before, a living entity develops a sort of complexity by material association, and the illusory encagement of the material body is accepted as an actual fact. Under such false complexity, the living beings under different categories of life become illusioned in different ways. Even in the most developed stage of human life, the same illusion prevails in the form of many *isms* and divides the loving relation with the Lord and thereby divides the loving relation between man and man. By hearing the subject matter of *Śrīmad-Bhāgavatam* this false complexity of materialism is removed, and real peace in society begins, which politicians aspire for so eagerly in so many political situations. The politicians want a peaceful situation between man and man, and nation and nation, but at the same time, because of too much attachment for material domination, there is illusion and fearfulness. Therefore the politicians' peace conferences cannot bring about peace in society. It can only be done by hearing the subject matter described in the *Śrīmad-Bhāgavatam* about the Supreme Personality of Godhead Śrī Kṛṣṇa. The foolish politicians may go on holding peace and summit conferences for hundreds of years, but they will fail to achieve success. Until we reach the stage of reestablishing our lost relation with Kṛṣṇa, the illusion of accepting the body as the self will prevail, and thus fearfulness will also prevail. As for the validity of Śrī Kṛṣṇa as the Supreme Personality of Godhead, there are hundreds and thousands of evidences from revealed scriptures, and there are hundreds and thousands of evidences from personal experiences of devotees in various places like Vṛndāvana, Navadvīpa and Purī. Even in the *Kaumudī* dictionary the synonyms of Kṛṣṇa are given as the son of Yaśodā and the Supreme Personality of Godhead Parabrahman. The conclusion is that simply by hearing the Vedic literature *Śrīmad-Bhāgavatam*, one can have direct connection with the Supreme Personality of Godhead Śrī Kṛṣṇa, and thereby one can attain the highest perfection of life by transcending worldly miseries, illusion and fearfulness. These are practical tests for one who has actually given a submissive hearing to the readings of the *Śrīmad-Bhāgavatam*.

Kṛṣṇa says that this special prerogative of the human being is not awakened very easily, except by some good association. Just as we have this Kṛṣṇa conscious association. If we attain such association, where nice things are discussed, then that awakening of reason, that special prerogative of the human being, will come. As long as this question does not arise in one's mind, he should understand that whatever activities he is doing will lead to his defeat. He is simply leading an animal life. But, not when these questions arise: Why am I suffering? What am I? Am I meant for suffering? Am I meant for troubles?

I am undergoing troubles by nature's laws, and by the state's laws. So the question of freedom is how to become free from all these troubles. The *Vedānta-sūtra* also says that the soul, my actual self, is by nature joyful. Yet, I am suffering. Lord Kṛṣṇa further says that when these questions arise, gradually one comes to God. Those who have awakened to these questions are said to lie on the path of perfection. And, when the question of God and our relationship with God comes, that is our final perfection of life.

Now, Kṛṣṇa says that out of many thousands of people, one may try to make perfection of this life; and out of many millions of such persons on the path of perfection, only one may understand Kṛṣṇa. So understanding Kṛṣṇa is not very easy. But it is also the easiest. It is not easy, but at the same time it is the easiest. It is the easiest if you follow the prescribed forms.

Lord Caitanya Mahāprabhu has introduced this chanting of Hare Kṛṣṇa. He has not exactly introduced it; it is in the scriptures. But He has especially propagated this formula. In this age this is the easiest method of self-realization. Simply chant Hare Kṛṣṇa. It can be done by everyone. In my classroom, I am perhaps the only Indian. My students are all Americans, and they are taking part in the chanting very nicely, chanting and dancing. That means that, in any country, in any place, this can be performed. Therefore it is the easiest. You may not understand the philosophy of the *Bhagavad-gītā*. That is also not very difficult; but still, if you think that you cannot understand, you can still chant very easily: Hare Kṛṣṇa, Hare Kṛṣṇa.

Understanding Subtle Science

Kṛṣṇa says that out of many millions of people, one may understand Him. But, by chanting of this Hare Kṛṣṇa, as introduced by Lord Caitanya—chanting and dancing—you can understand Kṛṣṇa within a very short time. Knowledge begins not from Kṛṣṇa, but from things which we are accustomed to see every day.

Land is gross. If you touch it, you can feel its hardness. But, as soon as the land becomes still finer, it is water, and the touch is soft. And then again, from water to fire, still finer. After fire or electricity the air is still finer; and after air, the sky, ether, is finer still. Beyond ether, the mind is still finer; and beyond the mind, intelligence is still finer. And, if you go beyond intelligence to understand the soul, it is finer still. From these elements people have discovered so many sciences. There are many scientists, for example, who are soil experts; they can say, by analyzing a particular type of earth, what kind of minerals are there. Somebody seeks out silver, somebody seeks out gold, somebody seeks out mica. This is knowledge of gross things—the earth. If you go to finer substances, then you study water, or liquid things, such as petrol and alcohol. Go still finer, and from water you will go to fire and electricity. If you study electricity, you have to study all sorts of books. And, from this finer fire, you will come to air. We have so much advancement in our airplanes; we are studying how they move, how they are made—now sputniks and jets—so many things are being discovered.

Next comes the study of the ethereal: electronics, ethereal transformations from one thing to another. Then, finer still, is the mind-psychology and psychiatry. But for intelligence, rationalism, there is only a little philosophical speculation. And what about the soul? Is there any science of the soul? The materialists have none. Material science has advanced to the study of the ether, or the mind and intelligence, but there is no advancement beyond that. Beyond intelligence, they do not know what exists. But here in the *Bhagavad-gītā* you can find this.

The *Bhagavad-gītā* begins at the point after intelligence. When Arjuna was perplexed at the outset, his intelligence was perplexed—whether to fight or not to fight. Kṛṣṇa begins the *Bhagavad-gītā* from the point where intelligence fails. How does knowledge of the soul begin? It is just like a child is playing. You can understand this child's body is now so small, but one day this child will be grown up, like you or me. But the same soul will continue. So, by intelligence, you can understand that although the body is changed, the soul is there. The same soul which was existing in the body of the child is still continuing in the body of the old man. Therefore the soul is permanent, and only the body has changed. This is a very easy thing to understand. And the last change of this body is death. As at every moment, every second, every day, every hour, the body is changing, so the last change is when one cannot act with the body, and so he has to take another one. Just as, when my cloth is too worn out or old, I cannot put it on; I have to take a new cloth. It is similar with the soul. When the body is too old or unworkable, I have to change to another body. This is called death.

This is the beginning of the *Bhagavad-gītā*, when the preliminary knowledge of the soul is there. And you will find that there are only a few who can understand the existence of the soul as permanent, and of the body as changeable. Therefore *Bhagavān*, Lord Kṛṣṇa, says that, out of many, many millions of people, one may understand it. But still, the knowledge is there. If you want to understand it, it is not difficult. You can understand it.

Now, we should inquire into the existence of the ego, the finest material substance. What is ego? I am pure soul, but with my intelligence and mind I am in contact with matter, and I have identified myself with matter. This is false ego. I am pure soul, but I am identifying falsely. For example, I am identifying with the land, thinking that I am Indian, or that I am American. This is called *ahaṅkāra* or false ego. *Ahaṅkāra* means the point where the pure soul touches matter. That junction is called *ahaṅkāra*. *Ahaṅkāra* is still finer than intelligence.

Kṛṣṇa says that these are the eight material elements: earth, water, fire, air, ether, mind, intelligence and false ego. False ego means false identification. Our nescient life has begun from this false identification—thinking that I am this matter, although I am seeing every day, at every moment, that I am not this matter. The soul is permanently existing, while matter is changing. This misconception, this illusion, is called *ahaṅkāra*, false ego. And your liberation means when you are out of this false ego. What is that status? *Ahaṁ brahmāsmi.* I am Brahman, I am spirit. That is the beginning of liberation.

Of course, one may be suffering from disease, from fever, and the temperature may come down to normal, 98.6 degrees. So he is now normal, but that is not the cure. Suppose for two days he has a 98.6 degree temperature, but with a slight change of diet, a slight change of behavior, the temperature rises immediately to 100. Relapse. Similarly, simply purifying the mind, rejecting this false *ahaṅkāra* identification—I am not this body, I am not this matter; I am soul—this is not liberation. It is only the beginning of liberation. If you stick to this point, and continue—just as you might continue your activities and keep your temperature at 98.6 degrees—then you are a healthy man.

For example, in the West now there is some propaganda for taking intoxication. The people want to forget the bodily existence. But how long will you forget? There will be a relapse. You can forget for one hour or two, by intoxication, and think that I am not this body. But unless you are actually on the platform of understanding yourself by knowledge, it is not possible to continue. Still, everyone is trying to think, "I am not this body." They have experience that they are suffering so much on account of bodily identification, and so, "If only I could forget my bodily identification!"

This is only a negative conception. When you actually realize yourself, simply understanding that you are *Brahman* will not do. You have to engage in the activities of *Brahman*. Otherwise you will fall down. Simply flying very high is no solution to the problem of going to the moon. Nowadays the fools are trying to go to the moon, but they simply go 240,000 miles up from the Earth, touch the moon, and return. They are very proud. There is so much talk of aeronautics: crowds and meetings and conferences. But what have they done? What are 240,000 miles in that vast sky? If you go 240 million miles, still you are limited. So this will not do. If you want to go high, you must have permanent shelter. If you can take rest there, then you cannot fall down. But if you have no rest, then you will have to fall down. The airplane goes high, seven miles, eight miles up from the earth, but it comes down immediately.

So, simply understanding *ahaṅkāra* means no more than understanding the false identification. Simply understanding that I am not matter, I am soul, is not perfection. The impersonalist, the void philosopher, simply thinks of the negative, that I am not this matter, I am not this body. This will not stay. You have to not only realize that you are not matter, but you have to engage yourself in the spiritual world. And that spiritual world means to be working in Kṛṣṇa consciousness. That spiritual world, that functioning of our real life, is Kṛṣṇa consciousness.

False ego I have already explained. It is neither matter nor spirit, but the junction—where the spirit soul comes into contact with matter and forgets himself. It is just as, in delirium, a man is diseased and his brain becomes puzzled, and gradually he forgets himself and becomes a madman. He is gradually forgetting. So there is the beginning of loss, and there is one point where he forgets. That beginning point is called *ahaṅkāra*, or false ego.

Chanting the *mahā-mantra*—Hare Kṛṣṇa, Hare Kṛṣṇa, Kṛṣṇa Kṛṣṇa, Hare Hare/ Hare Rāma, Hare Rāma, Rāma Rāma, Hare Hare—is the process not merely of putting an end to this false conception of the self, but it goes beyond that, to the point where the pure spirit soul engages in his eternal, blissful, all-knowing activities in the loving service of God. This is the height of conscious development, the ultimate goal of all living entities now evolving through the cycles and species of material nature.

Transcending Transmigration

So our problems of life, as it is stated in the *Bhagavad-gītā*, are to solve these four things: birth, old age, disease and death. No more birth.... Always remember that we are all eternal. Just like in this body, beginning from my mother's womb up to this old age, I am the same eternal soul, but my body is changing. So after changing this body also, I shall remain the same. Simply I shall have another body. This plain truth, there is no difficulty to understand. This is very nicely illustrated by these verses from the *Bhagavad-gītā*:

dehino 'smin yathā dehe
kaumāraṁ yauvanaṁ jarā
tathā dehāntara-prāptir
dhīras tatra na muhyati

(Bhagavad-gītā 2.13)

TRANSLATION

As the embodied soul continuously passes, in this body, from boyhood to youth to old age, the soul similarly passes into another body at death. A sober person is not bewildered by such a change.

na jāyate mriyate vā kadācin
nāyaṁ bhūtvā bhavitā vā na bhūyaḥ
ajo nityaḥ śāśvato 'yaṁ purāṇo
na hanyate hanyamāne śarīre

(Bhagavad-gītā 2.20)

TRANSLATION

For the soul there is neither birth nor death at any time. He has not come into being, does not come into being, and will not come into being. He is unborn, eternal, ever-existing and primeval. He is not slain when the body is slain.

vāsāṁsi jīrṇāni yathā vihāya
navāni gṛhṇāti naro 'parāṇi
tathā śarīrāṇi vihāya jīrṇāny
anyāni saṁyāti navāni dehī
(Bhagavad-gītā 2.22)

TRANSLATION

As a person puts on new garments, giving up old ones, the soul similarly accepts new material bodies, giving up the old and useless ones.

Now if I am eternal... If I am eternal means no death, no birth, no disease, no old age. That is eternal. So if I am eternal, whether it is possible to get an eternal body? Or eternal happiness? That is the problem of human society. If you can solve that problem, then you be proud of your civilization. Otherwise there is no difference between cats' and dogs' civilization and your civilization because you are simply trying to solve the problems of eating, sleeping, defending and mating. But these problems are already solved by nature's law.

Everyone is trying to be perfect. The whole struggle of existence is going on all over the world, how to become perfect. So that perfection ideal is different for different persons. Somebody is thinking that "If I have a nice bungalow and a nice bank balance and nice wife and children and family, then my life is perfect." Somebody is thinking that "If I can make my country very happy in comparison to other countries, then it is happy..." So there are different types of perfection. But actual perfection is... They do not know. That is indicated, that I am... Because I have been described, I am the soul. I am not this body. Dehino 'smin yatha dehe (Bhagavad-gītā 2.13). Within this body there is the *dehi*. *Dehi* means the proprietor of this body. So that *dehi*, he is, *tatha dehantara-praptih*, he is changing from one body to another. Just like we have got experience in this life also, from childhood to boyhood, boyhood to youthhood. As we are changing, past and present, therefore after this body is annihilated, *na hanyate hanyamane sarire* (Bhagavad-gītā 2.20), I am not annihilated; I take another body. That body... What kind of body? That will depend on my work.

Just like you are infected with some disease, nature's law is that you must suffer from that disease. Nature's law is like that. If you take more food than you can digest... Then immediately there will be dysentery. This is nature's law. If you take more than you can digest, then immediately there will be indigestion, means you cannot assimilate so much food. That is nature's law. If you touch fire, either you touch or your innocent child touches, the fire will burn it. Fire will not consider that "Here is a child. Let me excuse." No, it will burn. This is nature's law. Similarly, the thoughts which you are maintaining during your lifetime, if that thought becomes prominent—naturally it becomes—at the time of death, then you are going to get a similar body. If you are thinking like a demon, then you get the demon's body next life. And if you are thinking like a devotee, then you get your next life back to home, back to Godhead. This is nature's law.

Therefore, if you practice instead of thinking like the demons, how to gratify senses... That is the demonic thought. They are concerned with this body. If you think of Kṛṣṇa, how to serve Him, that is your perfection of life. Thinking at the time of death of Kṛṣṇa—*ante nārāyaṇa-smṛtih*—that is the perfection of life. *Ante*, at the time of death, if you remember Kṛṣṇa, then your life is successful. *Tyaktva deham punar janma naiti mam eti kaunteya* (Bhagavad-gītā 4.9). So we have to do like that, not like the *asurā*s or demons. Thinking must be there, but if you think of this body—how to keep it very comfortably, how to enjoy senses, how to have more money, how to have more men or women, how to see naked dance, how to do, how to this, how to this—then you are demon. And at the time of death, naturally we shall think of. Then I get again demonic life or animal life or tree life. So, as we are creating our mentality by different types of activities, our next life will be according to that mentality. This is the law of nature. *Śrīmad Bhāgavatam* illustrates this point very clearly:

parābhavas tāvad abodha-jāto
yāvan na jijñāsata ātma-tattvam
yāvat kriyās tāvad idaṁ mano vai
karmātmakaṁ yena śarīra-bandhaḥ

(Śrīmad-Bhāgavatam 5.5.5)

TRANSLATION

As long as one does not inquire about the spiritual values of life, one is defeated and subjected to miseries arising from ignorance. Be it sinful or pious, *karma* has its resultant actions. If a person is engaged in any kind of *karma*, his mind is called *karmātmaka*, colored with fruitive activity. As long as the mind is impure, consciousness is unclear, and as long as one is absorbed in fruitive activity, he has to accept a material body.

But we do not have this information. *prakṛteḥ kriyamāṇāni guṇaiḥ karmāṇi sarvaśaḥ* (Bhagavad-gītā 3.27). Actually, *prakrti*, nature, is pulling us according to our desire. The desire is contamination, the mental contamination. And we are creating different types of body. So our real suffering is the transmigration from one body to another. That we do not know. But it is stated in the *Bhagavad-gītā*, *tathā dehāntara-prāptiḥ*. You have to accept. And that is explained in other places, in *Srimad-Bhāgavatam. karmaṇā daiva-netreṇa jantur dehopapattaye* (Śrīmad-Bhāgavatam 5.5.5) . In the *Bhagavad-gītā* it is also stated, *yaṁ yaṁ vāpi smaran bhāvaṁ tyajaty ante kalevaram* (Bhagavad-gītā 8.6). At the time of your death, the situation which you have created, it will carry you. Because mind is there. Mind is subtle. Intelligence is subtle. That mind, intelligence and ego. The subtle body is there. The gross body is lost. But the subtle body will take you to another gross body. It will take to the womb of another mother. And according to your *karma*, by the mother's help you will get a body, and duly you will come out and begin your work. This is nature's process. It is going on.

prakṛteḥ kriyamāṇāni
guṇaiḥ karmāṇi sarvaśaḥ
ahaṅkāra-vimūḍhātmā
kartāham iti manyate
(Bhagavad-gītā 3.27)

Ahankara. But one who is puffed up with false ego, that "I am this," "I am that," "I am big man," "I am small man," but he does not know how *prakrti* is working... You may be very big man in this life. That does not mean that you will remain a big man in the next life. Suppose you are prime minister, but if you have contaminated some disease, you must suffer. It is not that nature will excuse you, "Oh, you are prime minister. You have infected this disease, and you will not suffer." No. You have to. So it is the question of creating the mind, the intelligence. Therefore if you constantly keep yourself, your mind, absorbed in Krsna, then you get next time, next life, a body like Krsna, which means *sac-cid-ānanda-vigraha. īśvaraḥ paramaḥ kṛṣṇaḥ sac-cid-ānanda-vigrahaḥ* (Brahma saṁhitā 5.1).

So, you must scrutinizingly try to understand the mercy of Lord Caitanya, this Krsna consciousness movement and how it is solving the problems of our life. *Vicāra karile citte pābe camatkāra.* If you scrutinizingly test it and try to understand this movement, then you'll feel yourself that it is wonderful. And actually it is wonderful and the process is also very simple. You do not require to be highly educated or philosopher or talented or rich or poor, or black and white. Doesn't matter what you are. It is universal. Any human being with little intelligence, he can understand. And even he does not understand, this process is so nice that if you continue this process for a few weeks you'll be able to understand. This chanting of *Hare Kṛṣṇa, Hare Kṛṣṇa, Kṛṣṇa Kṛṣṇa, Hare Hare/ Hare Rāma, Hare Rāma, Rāma Rāma, Hare Hare* is transcendental vibration, sound. Sound is the origin of all creation. So this transcendental sound, if you vibrate, you will understand very quickly this philosophy of Kṛṣṇa consciousness. And there is no loss on your part. Suppose you chant Hare Kṛṣṇa; you do not lose anything. But if there is any gain, why don't you try it? We simply request you with folded hands that you kindly chant Hare Kṛṣṇa. We are simply requesting you. We're not asking you to pay us something or to suffer something or be educated or be engineer or be lawyer, then come to us. Never mind what you are. Stay in your position. Simply try to chant these sixteen words, *Hare Kṛṣṇa, Hare Kṛṣṇa, Kṛṣṇa Kṛṣṇa, Hare Hare/ Hare Rāma, Hare Rāma, Rāma Rāma, Hare Hare*. You can try for one week. And there is no hard and fast rules. You can chant anywhere and everywhere. While walking you can chant, while driving you can chant. Nobody is going to tax, that "You are chanting. Give me this tax." It is very easy.

So *kirtaniyah sada harih . Ceto-darpana-marjanam.* If you chant, the result will be that your mind will be cleansed. The whole misunderstanding is that "I am not this body. I am spirit soul. But I am identifying myself with this—'I am Indian,' 'I am American,' 'I am Christian,' 'I am Hindu.'" These are all your designations. You are spirit soul. Just try to understand that you are spirit soul, and try to understand on the platform of spiritual understanding. All problems will be solved. And so long you are standing on this designated platform—"I am American," "I am Indian," "I am this," "I am that"—there is no solution of problems. Take it for granted. There is no solution of problem. You stand on this platform of spiritual understanding; there will be solution of all problems. This is authentic, and those who have followed, they have got result. Simply chant *Hare Kṛṣṇa, Hare Kṛṣṇa, Kṛṣṇa Kṛṣṇa, Hare Hare/ Hare Rāma, Hare Rāma, Rāma Rāma, Hare Hare*, and see the result practically. With my request, you can chant for one week and see the result.

This Hare Kṛṣṇa, this vibration may be foreign to you, but there is no difficulty to chant. The words may be in Sanskrit, but it is not difficult to chant. And if you simply chant, you get the result because it is transcendental vibration. Just like when television or radio vibration is there, either in India, America, everywhere the vibration is equally beneficial. Similarly, this transcendental vibration is coming down from the transcendental world. It is not material sound. It is not hackneyed. If you chant, if you practice, you'll realize it. So our request is that without any charges, without any fee, without any bluff, we say that you please chant *Hare Kṛṣṇa, Hare Kṛṣṇa, Kṛṣṇa Kṛṣṇa, Hare Hare/ Hare Rāma, Hare Rāma, Rāma Rāma, Hare Hare.*

Kṛṣṇa says *man-manā bhava mad-bhakto mad-yājī māṁ namaskuru* (Bhagavad-gītā 18.65). This is the process. *Man-manaḥ*: "You always think of Me." And we say, "Chant Hare Kṛṣṇa." *Hare Kṛṣṇa, Hare Kṛṣṇa, Kṛṣṇa Kṛṣṇa, Hare Hare/ Hare Rāma, Hare Rāma, Rāma Rāma, Hare Hare.* If you chant somebody's name, your friend's name or your relative's, immediately you remember the person. It is not very difficult. If you hear in the telephone somebody speaking, as soon as you hear the voice, you can understand, the other side, the person is there. So the chanting process means to always think of Kṛṣṇa, twenty-four hours. Caitanya Mahāprabhu advises *kīrtanīyaḥ sadā hariḥ* (Caitanya caritāmṛta. Adi 17.31). And what is the benefit? The benefit is, because Kṛṣṇa is the supreme pure, you become purified. Just like if you remain with the fire, you become warm, warmer, warmer, warmer. Just like in the fire you put one iron rod. It becomes warmer, warmer. At the end the iron rod becomes red-hot. And when it is red-hot, it is no more iron rod; it is fire. You touch everywhere; it will burn. The same process. If you remain with Kṛṣṇa always, you get Kṛṣṇa's quality. You have got the quality because you are part and parcel of Kṛṣṇa. If Kṛṣṇa is gold, you are part and parcel of Kṛṣṇa; therefore you are also gold. But at the present moment, as the gold is covered by dirt, at the present moment we are spirit soul, we are part and parcel of Kṛṣṇa, as good as Kṛṣṇa, but we have been covered by this material body. Therefore we have to take out ourself from this material body. That is called *siddhi*, that is called perfection.

Section III

Towards Perfect Peace & Happiness

āpūryamāṇam acala-pratiṣṭhaṁ
samudram āpaḥ praviśanti yadvat
tadvat kāmā yaṁ praviśanti sarve
sa śāntim āpnoti na kāma-kāmī

(Bhagavad-gītā 2.70)

TRANSLATION

A person who is not disturbed by the incessant flow of desires—that enter like rivers into the ocean, which is ever being filled but is always still—can alone achieve peace, and not the man who strives to satisfy such desires.

PURPORT

Although the vast ocean is always filled with water, it is always, especially during the rainy season, being filled with much more water. But the ocean remains the same—steady; it is not agitated, nor does it cross beyond the limit of its brink. That is also true of a person fixed in Kṛṣṇa consciousness. As long as one has the material body, the demands of the body for sense gratification will continue. The devotee, however, is not disturbed by such desires, because of his fullness. A Kṛṣṇa conscious man is not in need of anything, because the Lord fulfills all his material necessities. Therefore he is like the ocean—always full in himself. Desires may come to him like the waters of the rivers that flow into the ocean, but he is steady in his activities, and he is not even slightly disturbed by desires for sense gratification. That is the proof of a Kṛṣṇa conscious man—one who has lost all inclinations for material sense gratification, although the desires are present. Because he remains satisfied in the transcendental loving service of the Lord, he can remain steady, like the ocean, and therefore enjoy full peace. Others, however, who want to fulfill desires even up to the limit of liberation, what to speak of material success, never attain peace. The fruitive workers, the salvationists, and also the *yogīs* who are after mystic powers are all unhappy because of unfulfilled desires. But the person in Kṛṣṇa consciousness is happy in the service of the Lord, and he has no desires to be fulfilled. In fact, he does not even desire liberation from the so-called material bondage. The devotees of Kṛṣṇa have no material desires, and therefore they are in perfect peace.

CHAPTER 4

The Real Peace Formula

Every living entity is searching after peace. That is the struggle for existence. Everyone, from the aquatics to the highest form of human being—from the ant up to Brahmā, the first creature of this universe—is searching for peace. That is the main objective. Lord Caitanya said that a person who is in full Kṛṣṇa consciousness is the only peaceful man because he has no demands. That is the special qualification of a person who is in Kṛṣṇa consciousness. He is *akāmaḥ. Akāmaḥ* refers to those who have no desire, who are self-sufficient, who have nothing to ask and who are fully peaceful. Who are they? They are the devotees who are situated in Kṛṣṇa consciousness. The *Bhagavad-gītā* tells us about how being connected with the Supreme Lord brings about peace and happiness:

nāsti buddhir ayuktasya
na cāyuktasya bhāvanā
na cābhāvayataḥ śāntir
aśāntasya kutaḥ sukham

(Bhagavad-gītā 2.66)

TRANSLATION

One who is not connected with the Supreme [in Kṛṣṇa consciousness] can have neither transcendental intelligence nor a steady mind, without which there is no possibility of peace. And how can there be any happiness without peace?

PURPORT

Unless one is in Kṛṣṇa consciousness, there is no possibility of peace. So it is confirmed in the Fifth Chapter (5.29) that when one understands that Kṛṣṇa is the only enjoyer of all the good results of sacrifice and penance, that He is the proprietor of all universal manifestations, and that He is the real friend of all living entities, then only can one have real peace. Therefore, if one is not in Kṛṣṇa consciousness, there cannot be a final goal for the mind. Disturbance is due to want of an ultimate goal, and when one is certain that Kṛṣṇa is the enjoyer, proprietor and friend of everyone and everything, then one can, with a steady mind, bring about peace. Therefore, one who is engaged without a relationship with Kṛṣṇa is certainly always in distress and is without peace, however much he may make a show of peace and spiritual advancement in life. Kṛṣṇa consciousness is a self-manifested peaceful condition which can be achieved only in relationship with Kṛṣṇa.

Apart from the devotees of the Lord, everybody in this world falls into three classes. One class is *bhukti*, those who are hankering after material happiness and enjoyment. These people want to eat, drink, be merry and enjoy. There are different modes of enjoyment according to the body. People are searching after sense enjoyment on this planet, on other planets, here, there and everywhere. Their main object is to gratify the senses. That is called *bhukti*. The next class is those people who are fatigued or frustrated in sense gratification and therefore want liberation from this material entanglement. And then there are those who, in search of knowledge, speculate about what the Absolute Truth is. Thus there are some who want sense enjoyment, and others, the salvationists, who are seeking liberation. The salvationists also have some desire, the desire to be free from this material entanglement. Then there are those who are *yogīs*; they are searching after mystic perfection. There are eight kinds of mystic perfection which grant the ability to become the smallest, to become the heaviest, or to get whatever one desires. Ordinary persons who are after sense gratification and those who are salvationists or who are after mystic perfection all have some demand. But what about the devotees? They have no demands. Because they simply want to serve Kṛṣṇa, they are waiting for the order of Kṛṣṇa, and that is their satisfaction. If Kṛṣṇa wants the devotees to go to hell, they are prepared to go to hell. And if Kṛṣṇa says, "You come to Me," they are prepared to go. They have no demands. This is the perfectional stage.

There is a very nice verse in which a devotee prays: "I shall simply be conscious of You, my dear Lord, Kṛṣṇa conscious, free from all mental demands." Actually, because we are in material bondage, we have many demands. Some people want sense gratification, those who are a little more elevated want mental satisfaction, and those who are still more refined want to show some magic jugglery of power in this world. They are all in material bondage in different capacities. Therefore, a person who is Kṛṣṇa conscious prays to the Lord: "My dear Lord, when shall I be fully absorbed in Your thoughts or Your service?" "Your thoughts" are not simply abstract, concocted speculation; it is a practical mode of thought. "I shall become peaceful." All mental concoction—I want this, I want that—will be completely eradicated.

We are hovering over the mental plane. We have given power of attorney to the mind, and the mind is driving us—"Come here, go there." One has to stop such nonsense. "I shall simply be Your eternal servitor. And I shall be very cheerful, for I have my master." All others who are not in Kṛṣṇa consciousness are guideless. They are their own guides. The person who is Kṛṣṇa conscious has the supreme guide; therefore, he has no fear. For example, as long as a child is under the care of his parents he has no fear. But as soon as he becomes free, he finds many impediments. This is a crude example, but similarly, when one becomes completely free from all mental concoction and engages one hundred percent in Kṛṣṇa consciousness twenty-four hours a day, he will be peaceful at once. That is peace.

Therefore, Caitanya Mahāprabhu says that those who are Kṛṣṇa conscious, because they have no demands, are actually peaceful. The *Bhagavad-gītā* says in this regard:

vihāya kāmān yaḥ sarvān
pumāṁś carati niḥspṛhaḥ
nirmamo nirahaṅkāraḥ
sa śāntim adhigacchati

(Bhagavad-gītā 2.71)

TRANSLATION

A person who has given up all desires for sense gratification, who lives free from desires, who has given up all sense of proprietorship and is devoid of false ego—he alone can attain real peace.

PURPORT

To become desireless means not to desire anything for sense gratification. In other words, desire for becoming Kṛṣṇa conscious is actually desirelessness. To understand one's actual position as the eternal servitor of Kṛṣṇa, without falsely claiming this material body to be oneself and without falsely claiming proprietorship over anything in the world, is the perfect stage of Kṛṣṇa consciousness.

One who is situated in this perfect stage knows that because Kṛṣṇa is the proprietor of everything, everything must be used for the satisfaction of Kṛṣṇa. Arjuna did not want to fight for his own sense satisfaction, but when he became fully Kṛṣṇa conscious he fought because Kṛṣṇa wanted him to fight. For himself there was no desire to fight, but for Kṛṣṇa the same Arjuna fought to his best ability. Real desirelessness is desire for the satisfaction of Kṛṣṇa, not an artificial attempt to abolish desires. The living entity cannot be desireless or senseless, but he does have to change the quality of the desires. A materially desireless person certainly knows that everything belongs to Kṛṣṇa (*īśāvāsyam idaṁ sarvam*), and therefore he does not falsely claim proprietorship over anything. This transcendental knowledge is based on self-realization—namely, knowing perfectly well that every living entity is an eternal part and parcel of Kṛṣṇa in spiritual identity, and that the eternal position of the living entity is therefore never on the level of Kṛṣṇa or greater than Him. This understanding of Kṛṣṇa consciousness is the basic principle of real peace.

Those who are after sense enjoyment, salvation and yogic mystic perfection are always full of anxiety. As long as one is full of anxiety, one should know that he is still under the grip of material nature. And as soon as one is free from all anxiety, one should know that he is liberated. This fearful anxiety exists because we do not know Kṛṣṇa, the Supreme Lord, the supreme controller. Instead, we have other conceptions, and therefore we are always anxious.

Everyone wants peace in the world. The peace marchers do not know how to obtain peace, but they want peace. I read a speech of the Archbishop of Canterbury in which he said, "You want the kingdom of God without God." This is our defect. If you want peace at all, then accept that peace means to understand

God. That is stated in the *Bhagavad-gītā*. Unless you are in touch with the Supreme Lord, Kṛṣṇa, you cannot have peace. Therefore, we have a different peace formula. The real peace formula is that one must know that God is the proprietor of all this universe, including the United States of America. He is the proprietor of Russia, He is the proprietor of China, He is the proprietor of India, of everything. But because we claim that we are the proprietors, there is fighting, there is discord, there is disagreement, and how can there be peace?

bhoktāraṁ yajña-tapasāṁ
sarva-loka-maheśvaram
suhṛdaṁ sarva-bhūtānāṁ
jñātvā māṁ śāntim ṛcchati

(Bhagavad-gītā 5.29)

TRANSLATION

A person in full consciousness of Me, knowing Me to be the ultimate beneficiary of all sacrifices and austerities, the Supreme Lord of all planets and demigods, and the benefactor and well-wisher of all living entities, attains peace from the pangs of material miseries.

PURPORT

The conditioned souls within the clutches of the illusory energy are all anxious to attain peace in the material world. But they do not know the formula for peace, which is explained in this part of the *Bhagavad-gītā*. The greatest peace formula is simply this: Lord Kṛṣṇa is the beneficiary in all human activities. Men should offer everything to the transcendental service of the Lord because He is the proprietor of all planets and the demigods thereon. No one is greater than He. He is greater than the greatest of the demigods, Lord Śiva and Lord Brahmā. In the *Vedas* (*Śvetāś-*

vatara Upaniṣad 6.7) the Supreme Lord is described as *tam īś-varāṇāṁ paramaṁ maheśvaram.* Under the spell of illusion, living entities are trying to be lords of all they survey, but actually they are dominated by the material energy of the Lord. The Lord is the master of material nature, and the conditioned souls are under the stringent rules of material nature. Unless one understands these bare facts, it is not possible to achieve peace in the world either individually or collectively. This is the sense of Kṛṣṇa consciousness: Lord Kṛṣṇa is the supreme predominator, and all living entities, including the great demigods, are His subordinates. One can attain perfect peace only in complete Kṛṣṇa consciousness.

This Fifth Chapter is a practical explanation of Kṛṣṇa consciousness, generally known as *karma-yoga*. The question of mental speculation as to how *karma-yoga* can give liberation is answered herewith. To work in Kṛṣṇa consciousness is to work with the complete knowledge of the Lord as the predominator. Such work is not different from transcendental knowledge. Direct Kṛṣṇa consciousness is *bhakti-yoga*, and *jñāna-yoga* is a path leading to *bhakti-yoga.* Kṛṣṇa consciousness means to work in full knowledge of one's relationship with the Supreme Absolute, and the perfection of this consciousness is full knowledge of Kṛṣṇa, or the Supreme Personality of Godhead. A pure soul is the eternal servant of God as His fragmental part and parcel. He comes into contact with *māyā* (illusion) due to the desire to lord it over *māyā*, and that is the cause of his many sufferings. As long as he is in contact with matter, he has to execute work in terms of material necessities. Kṛṣṇa consciousness, however, brings one into spiritual life even while one is within the jurisdiction of matter, for it is an arousing of spiritual existence by practice in the material world. The more one is advanced, the more he is freed from the clutches of matter. The Lord is not partial toward anyone. Everything depends on one's practical performance of duties in Kṛṣṇa consciousness, which helps one control the senses in every respect and conquer the influence of desire and anger. And one who stands fast in Kṛṣṇa consciousness, controlling the abovementioned passions, remains factually in the transcendental stage, or *brahma-nirvāṇa.* The eightfold yoga mysticism is automatically practiced in Kṛṣṇa consciousness because the ultimate purpose is served. There is a gradual process of elevation in the practice of *yama, niyama, āsana, prāṇāyāma, pratyāhāra, dhāraṇā, dhyāna* and *samādhi.* But these only preface perfection by devotional service, which alone can award peace to the human being. It is the highest perfection of life.

First of all, one has to accept that God is the proprietor of everything. We are simply guests for fifty or a hundred years. We come and go, and while one is here, he is absorbed in this thought: "This is my land. This is my family. This is my body. This is my property." And when there is an order from the Supreme for one to leave his home, his property, his body, his family, his money and his bank balance and it is all gone, one has to take another place. We are under the grip of material nature, and she is offering different kinds of bodies: "Now, my dear sir, you accept this body." We accept an American body, an Indian body, a Chinese body, a cat's body or a dog's body. I am not the Proprietor even of this body, yet I say that I am this body. Actually, this is ignorance. And how can one have peace? Peace can be had when one understands that God is the proprietor of everything. One's friends, one's mother, one's mother's father and the President are all guests of time. When this knowledge is accepted, then there will be peace.

We are searching for a friend to give us peace and tranquillity. That friend is Kṛṣṇa, God. Just make friendship with Him; you'll find everyone to be your friend. Because God is situated in everyone's heart, if you make friendship with God, He will dictate from within so that you will also be treated in a friendly way. If you make friendship with the police commissioner, you receive some advantage. If you make friendship with President Nixon, everyone will be your friend because everyone is under the President. If you want something from any officer, simply call President Nixon, and he will say, "All right, look after this man." Everything is taken care of. Just try to have friendship with God, and everyone will be your friend. If all people understand this very nice fact, that God is everyone's friend and that He is the supreme proprietor, they will become peaceful. That is explained also by Lord Caitanya.

In *Bhagavad-gītā*, *Śrīmad-Bhāgavatam*, *Caitanya-caritāmṛta*, or any Vedic literature or any other literature in any other religion, the same fact is presented: God is the proprietor. God is the only friend. If you understand this, then you'll have peace. This is the peace formula. As soon as you encroach on God's Property, calling it your own, material nature, the police action, will be there: "You are not the proprietor." You can simply have what is allotted to you by God. The following verses from the Vedic scriptures illustrate this principle:

ātmāvāsyam idaṁ viśvaṁ
yat kiñcij jagatyāṁ jagat
tena tyaktena bhuñjīthā
mā gṛdhaḥ kasya svid dhanam

(Śrīmad-Bhāgavatam 8.1.10)

TRANSLATION

Within this universe, the Supreme Personality of Godhead in His Supersoul feature is present everywhere, wherever there are animate or inanimate beings. Therefore, one should accept only that which is allotted to him; one should not desire to infringe upon the property of others.

īśāvāsyam idam sarvaṁ
yat kiñca jagatyāṁ jagat
tena tyaktena bhuñjīthā
mā gṛdhaḥ kasya svid dhanam

(Īśopaniṣad Mantra 1)

TRANSLATION

Everything animate or inanimate that is within the universe is controlled and owned by the Lord. One should therefore accept only those things necessary for himself, which are set aside as his quota, and one should not accept other things, knowing well to whom they belong.

Actually only those who are Kṛṣṇa conscious are peaceful, unafraid of anything. They are neither in heaven nor in hell nor anywhere but with Kṛṣṇa, so for them everything is Vaikuṇṭha, without fear. Similarly, Lord Kṛṣṇa as Paramātmā, Supersoul, lives everywhere. He lives in the heart of a hog also. The hog eats stool, but that does not mean that because the Supreme Lord is in the heart of the hog, He is also subjected to such punishment. The Lord and His devotees are always transcendental to the modes of material nature. Persons who are completely Kṛṣṇa conscious are very rare and very peaceful. Out of millions and millions of people, it is very difficult to find one who is actually Kṛṣṇa conscious; this position of Kṛṣṇa consciousness is so rare. But Kṛṣṇa Himself, as Lord Caitanya, seeing the pitiable condition of the present day, is directly giving free love of Godhead.

Yet because love of God is being given freely and so easily, people do not care for it. My spiritual master used to say that if you take a langera mango, which is a first-class, topmost quality mango in India, very costly, very sweet and very tasteful, and go from door to door and try to distribute it freely, people will doubt: "Why has this man brought this langera mango? Why is he trying to distribute it freely? There must be some motive behind it." Similarly, Lord Caitanya distributed this Kṛṣṇa consciousness langera mango very cheaply, but people are so foolish that they think, "Oh, they are simply chanting Hare Kṛṣṇa; what is there to it? This is meant for the foolish, who cannot speculate and do not have any higher standard of knowledge." But that is not so. It is said: "Out of millions and millions of people, only a few are interested in Kṛṣṇa consciousness." Do not neglect this information; it is very rare, and if you practice Kṛṣṇa consciousness, your life will be successful. Your mission in human life will be fulfilled. This seed of Kṛṣṇa consciousness is very rare and very valuable. Lord Caitanya said that innumerable living entities are wandering and transmigrating in the 8,400,000 species of life, one after another. Out of so many, one may come who is fortunate, who has spiritual fortune.

Kṛṣṇa is within you, and as soon as Kṛṣṇa sees that you are very sincere, that you are seeking, He sends a bona fide spiritual master. This combination of Kṛṣṇa and the spiritual master is the cause of one's receiving the seed of Kṛṣṇa consciousness. The seed is there. If you have a very nice seed of a rose bush, what is your duty? If you have a seed of any nice plant, it is your duty not to lock it up in the safety vault of a bank. Your duty is to sow it in the ground. Where should you sow that seed? If you have information of Kṛṣṇa consciousness, you just sow it in your heart. Not in this earth, but in the earth within yourself. And after sowing a seed you have to pour a little water on it, so that water is hearing and chanting. Once the seed is sown in the heart, just pour on a little water, and it will grow.

This process should not be stopped by the thought that because one is initiated there is no need of hearing and chanting. It should go on continuously. If you stop pouring water on a plant, it will dry up, it will not produce any fruit. Similarly, even if you are highly elevated in Kṛṣṇa consciousness, you cannot stop this process of hearing and chanting because *māyā* is so strong, so powerful, that as soon as she sees, "Ah, here is an opportunity," at once you will dry up. By the process of pouring water, that plant of Kṛṣṇa consciousness grows. How does it grow? There is a limit to every plant you see; it grows and grows and grows, but there is a limit where it stops growing. But the plant of Kṛṣṇa consciousness grows in such a way that it does not rest in any part of this material universe because a Kṛṣṇa conscious person is not satisfied with planetary facilities in any part of this material universe. Even if you offer him *Siddhaloka*, where the inhabitants are so powerful and elevated that they can fly in the sky without airplanes, he will not be satisfied.

There is a planet, *Siddhaloka*, according to *Śrīmad-Bhāgavatam*, where the inhabitants do not need airplanes or spacecraft to fly from one planet to another. Above *Siddhaloka* there are many other planets. I saw that the latest modern opinion is that every star is a sun, and there are different planetary systems, solar systems; but according to Vedic literature there are innumerable universes which are separate identities. The limit of this universe is the outermost sky. The modern scientist says that each and every star is a sun. But Vedic literature does not say that. Vedic literature informs us that there is only one sun in each universe, but there are innumerable universes, and thus there are innumerable suns and moons. The highest planet of this universe is called *Brahmaloka*. And Lord Kṛṣṇa says, "Even if you approach the highest planet, you have to come back again." Sputniks and astronauts are going very high, and here on earth people are clapping; but after just a brief time they come down again. However one may clap, he cannot do more than that. Similarly, those who are materialistic can go high up to *Brahmaloka* where *Brahmā* is, but those who are Kṛṣṇa conscious will reject even that. They neglect even the impersonal *brahmajyoti*. They don't care for it.

The covering of this universe is far, far greater than this space which we are now in. The outside of the universe is ten times the space within, so one has to penetrate that covering, and then reach *Virajā*, the Causal Ocean. The Buddhist philosophical perfection is to reach that *Virajā*. When this material existence is completely finished, it is called *virajā*, according to Vedic language. But the Kṛṣṇa conscious person not only penetrates the covering of this universe, but after he reaches that Causal Ocean, which is the neutral position, he continues. The plant grows so nicely from *Brahmaloka* to *Virajā* to the spiritual sky, and even when that plant reaches the spiritual sky, it is not satisfied with any *Vaikuṇṭha* planet.

The highest planet in the spiritual sky is *Kṛṣṇaloka*. It is just like a lotus flower, where Kṛṣṇa is standing. And there, when the plant finds Kṛṣṇa's lotus feet, it rests. Just as a creeper grows and grows and grows and at last attaches itself to something and then expands, when the devotional plant gets to the lotus feet of Kṛṣṇa, it expands. As soon as this Kṛṣṇa consciousness creeper captures Kṛṣṇa's lotus feet, it takes shelter. "There. Now I have finished my journey. Let me expand here." To expand means to enjoy Kṛṣṇa's association. There the devotees are satisfied.

That creeper has to go on, and thus those who are already in Kṛṣṇa consciousness, if they have their natural growth, relish the fruit of that creeper even in this life. If you continue this chanting and hearing process, you will grow and grow and actually reach Kṛṣṇa's lotus feet and there relish His association.

CHAPTER 5

Expanding Our Love

If you throw a stone into the middle of a pool of water, a circle will expand to the limit of the bank. Similarly, radio waves expand in a circle, and when you capture the waves with your radio you can hear the message. In the same way, our loving feeling can also expand.

At the beginning of our life, we simply want to eat. Whatever a small child grabs, he wants to eat. He has only personal interest. Then, when the child grows a little, he tries to participate with his brothers and sisters: "All right. You also take a little." This is an increase in the feeling of fellowship. Then, as he grows up, he begins to feel some love for his parents, then for his community, then for his country, and at last for all nations. But unless the center is right, that expansion of feeling—even if it is national or international—is not perfect.

For example, the meaning of the word national is "one who has taken birth in a particular country." You feel for other Americans because they are born in this country. You may even sacrifice your life for your countrymen. But there is a defect: If the definition of national is "one who is born in a particular country," then why are the animals born in America not considered Americans? The problem is that we are not expanding our feelings beyond the human society. Because we don't think animals are our countrymen, we send them to the slaughterhouse.

So the center of our national feeling or our international feeling is not fixed on the proper object. If the center is right, then you can draw any number of circles around that center and they'll never overlap. They'll simply keep growing, growing, growing. They'll not intersect with one another if the center is all right. Unfortunately, although everyone is feeling nationally or internationally, the center is missing. Therefore your international feeling and my international feeling, your national feeling and my national feeling, are overlapping and conflicting. So we have to find the proper center for our loving feelings. Then you can expand your circle of feelings and it will not overlap or conflict with others'.

That center is Kṛṣṇa.

yad yujyate 'su-vasu-karma-mano-vacobhir
dehātmajādiṣu nṛbhis tad asat pṛthaktvāt
tair eva sad bhavati yat kriyate 'pṛthaktvāt
sarvasya tad bhavati mūla-niṣecanaṁ yat

(Śrīmad-Bhāgavatam 8.9.29)

TRANSLATION

In human society there are various activities performed for the protection of one's wealth and life by one's words, one's mind and one's actions, but they are all performed for one's personal or extended sense gratification with reference to the body. All these activities are baffled because of being separate from devotional service. But when the same activities are performed for the satisfaction of the Lord, the beneficial results are distributed to everyone, just as water poured on the root of a tree is distributed throughout the entire tree.

PURPORT

This is the distinction between materialistic activities and activities performed in Kṛṣṇa consciousness. The entire world is active, and this includes the *karmīs*, the *jñānīs*, the *yogīs* and the *bhaktas*. However, all activities except those of the *bhaktas*, the devotees, end in bafflement and a waste of time and energy. *Moghāśā mogha-karmāṇo mogha jñānā vicetasaḥ:* if one is not a devotee, his hopes, his activities and his knowledge are all baffled. A nondevotee works for his personal sense gratification or for the sense gratification of his family, society, community or nation, but because all such activities are separate from the Supreme Personality of Godhead, they are considered *asat*. The word *asat* means bad or temporary, and *sat* means permanent and good. Activities performed for the satisfaction of Kṛṣṇa are permanent and good, but *asat* activity, although sometimes celebrated as philanthropy, altruism, nationalism, this "*ism*" or that "*ism*," will never produce any permanent result and is therefore all bad. Even a little work done in Kṛṣṇa consciousness is a permanent asset and is all-good because it is done for Kṛṣṇa, the all-good Supreme Personality of Godhead, who is everyone's friend *(suhṛdaṁ sarva-bhūtānām)*. The Supreme Personality of Godhead is the only enjoyer and proprietor of everything *(bhoktāraṁ yajña-tapasāṁ sarva-loka-maheśvaram)*. Therefore any activity performed for the Supreme Lord is permanent. As a result of such activities, the performer is immediately recognized. *Na ca tasmān manuṣyeṣu kaścin me priya-kṛttamaḥ.* Such a devotee, because of full knowledge of the Supreme Personality of Godhead, is immediately transcendental, although he may superficially appear to be engaged in materialistic activities. The only distinction between materialistic activity and spiritual activity is that material activity is performed only to satisfy one's own senses whereas spiritual activity is meant to satisfy the transcendental senses of the Supreme Personality of Godhead. By spiritual activity everyone factually benefits, whereas by materialistic activity no one benefits and instead one becomes entangled in the laws of karma.

Now we have expanded our feelings of love to various objects. We may love our country, we may love our community, we may love our family, we may love our cats and dogs. In any case, we have love, and we expand it according to our knowledge. And when our knowledge is perfect, we come to the point of loving Kṛṣṇa. That is perfection. Love of Kṛṣṇa is the aim of all activities, the aim of life.

The *Śrīmad-Bhāgavatam* (1.2.8) confirms that the goal of life is Kṛṣṇa:

dharmaḥ svanuṣṭhitaḥ puṁsāṁ
viṣvaksena-kathāsu yaḥ
notpādayed yadi ratiṁ
śrama eva hi kevalam

The first words in this verse are *dharmaḥ svanuṣṭhitaḥ puṁsām*. This means that everyone is doing his duty according to his position. A householder has some duty, a *sannyāsī* [renunciant] has some duty, a *brahmacārī* [celibate student] has some duty. There are different types of duties according to different occupations or professions. But, the *Bhāgavatam* says, if by performing your duties very nicely you still do not come to the understanding of Kṛṣṇa, then whatever you have done is simply useless labor (*śrama eva hi kevalam*). So if you want to come to the point of perfection, you should try to understand and love Kṛṣṇa. Then your national or international feelings of love will actually expand to their limit.

Now, suppose a man says, "Yes, I have expanded my feelings of love very widely." That is all right, but he must show the symptoms of how his feelings of love are expanded. As Kṛṣṇa says in the Bhagavad-gītā (5.18):

vidyā-vinaya-sampanne
brāhmaṇe gavi hastini

śuni caiva śvapāke ca
paṇḍitāḥ sama-darśinaḥ

If one is actually a *paṇḍita*, someone who is elevated to the stage of perfect wisdom, then he must see everyone on an equal platform (*sama-darśinaḥ*). Because the vision of a *paṇḍita* is no longer absorbed simply with the body, he sees a learned *brāhmaṇa* as a spirit soul, he sees a dog as a spirit soul, he sees an elephant as a spirit soul, and he also sees a lowborn man as a spirit soul. From the highborn *brāhmaṇa* down to the *caṇḍāla* [outcaste], there are many social classes in human society, but if a man is really learned he sees everyone, every living entity, on the same level. That is the stage of true learning.

We are trying to expand our feeling socially, communally, nationally, internationally, or universally. That is our natural function—to expand our consciousness. But my point is that if we actually want to expand our consciousness to the utmost, we must find out the real center of existence. That center is Kṛṣṇa, or God. How do we know Kṛṣṇa is God? Kṛṣṇa declares Himself to be God in the *Bhagavad-gītā*. Please always remember that the Kṛṣṇa consciousness movement is based on understanding *Bhagavad-gītā* as it is. Whatever I am speaking is in the *Bhagavad-gītā*. Unfortunately, the *Bhagavad-gītā* has been misinterpreted by so many commentators that people have misunderstood it. Actually, the purport of the *Bhagavad-gītā* is to develop Kṛṣṇa consciousness, love of Kṛṣṇa, and we are trying to teach that.

So Kṛṣṇa explains everything in the *Bhagavad-gītā*. And our purpose in the Kṛṣṇa consciousness movement is to spread the knowledge contained in the *Bhagavad-gītā* without adding any nonsensical commentary. Then the human society will profit from this knowledge. Now society is not in a sound condition, but if people understand the *Bhagavad-gītā*, and if they actually broaden their outlook, all social, national, and international problems will be solved automatically. There will be no difficulty. But if we don't find out what the center of existence is, if we manufacture our own ways to expand our loving feelings, there will be only conflict—not only between individual persons but between the different nations of the world. The nations are trying to be united; in your country there is the United Nations. Unfortunately, instead of the nations becoming united, the flags are increasing.

Instead of becoming united we are becoming disunited, because we are missing the center. Therefore, my request, since you are all international students, is that you please try to find out the real center of your international movement. Real international feeling will be possible when you understand that the center is Kṛṣṇa. Then your international movement will be perfect.

In the Fourteenth Chapter of Bhagavad-gītā (14.4), Lord Kṛṣṇa says,

sarva-yoniṣu kaunteya
mūrtayaḥ sambhavanti yāḥ
tāsāṁ brahma mahad yonir
ahaṁ bīja-pradaḥ pita

Here Kṛṣṇa says, "I am the father of all forms of life. The material nature is the mother, and I am the seed-giving father." Without a father and mother, nobody can be born. The father gives the seed, and the mother supplies the body. In this material world the mother of every one of us—from Lord Brahmā down to the ant—is the material nature. Our body is matter; therefore it is a gift of the material nature, our mother. But I, the spirit soul, am part and parcel of the supreme father, Kṛṣṇa. Kṛṣṇa says, *mamaivāṁśo... jīva-bhūtaḥ*: "All these living entities are part and parcel of Me."

Everybody in this world has got the propensity to love. Love means somebody else. Love cannot be done or love cannot be executed only one, personally. There must be another one. I love somebody; somebody loves me. So as soon as there is question of love, there must be lover, there must be beloved, and the transaction, then love. *Prema. Prema pum-artho mahan.* So we have got this loving propensity, to love somebody, to love my family. First of all, love begins from family— father, mother, brother, sister. Then you extend your love to your society, to your community, then to your nation. Or you can extend to the international. You can expand. But what is the end? You can expand yourself, but unless you come to the point of loving the Supreme Person, you cannot have tranquillity or peace of mind. That is the secret. Just like watering the tree. You can water, pour water on the leaves, on the branches, on the twigs, on the flowers, each and every one very particularly. But if you forget to water on the root, then everything is spoiled. Time is spoiled.

yathā taror mūla-niṣecanena
tṛpyanti tat-skandha-bhujopaśākhāḥ
prāṇopahārāc ca yathendriyāṇāṁ
tathaiva sarvārhaṇam acyutejyā

(Śrīmad-Bhāgavatam 4.31.14)

TRANSLATION

As pouring water on the root of a tree energizes the trunk, branches, twigs and everything else, and as supplying food to the stomach enlivens the senses and limbs of the body, simply worshiping the Supreme Personality of Godhead through devotional service automatically satisfies the demigods, who are parts of that Supreme Personality.

PURPORT

Sometimes people ask why this Kṛṣṇa consciousness movement simply advocates worship of Kṛṣṇa to the exclusion of the demigods. The answer is given in this verse. The example of pouring water on the root of a tree is very appropriate. In *Bhagavad-gītā* (15.1) it is said, *ūrdhva-mūlam adhaḥ-śākham:* this cosmic manifestation has expanded downward, and the root is the Supreme Personality of Godhead. As the Lord confirms in *Bhagavad-gītā* (10.8*), ahaṁ sarvasya prabhavaḥ:* "I am the source of all spiritual and material worlds." Kṛṣṇa is the root of everything; therefore rendering service to the Supreme Personality of Godhead, Kṛṣṇa (*kṛṣṇa-sevā*), means automatically serving all the demigods. Sometimes it is argued that *karma* and *jñāna* require a mixture of *bhakti* in order to be successfully executed, and sometimes it is argued that *bhakti* also requires *karma* and *jñāna* for its successful termination. The fact is, however, that although *karma* and *jñāna* cannot be successful without *bhakti, bhakti* does not require the help of *karma* and *jñāna*. Actually, as described by Śrīla Rūpa Gosvāmī, *anyābhilāṣitā-śūnyaṁ jñāna-karmādy-anāvṛtam:* pure devotional service should not be contaminated by the touch of *karma* and *jñāna*. Modern society is involved in various types of philanthropic works, humanitarian works and so on, but people do not know that these activities will never be successful unless Kṛṣṇa, the Supreme Personality of Godhead, is brought into the center. One may ask what harm there is in worshiping Kṛṣṇa and the different parts of His body, the demigods, and the answer is also given in this verse. The point is that by supplying food to the stomach, the *indriyas*, the senses, are automatically satisfied. If one tries to feed his eyes or ears independently, the result is only havoc. Simply by supplying food to the stomach, we satisfy all of the senses. It is neither necessary nor feasible to render separate service to the individual senses. The conclusion is that by serving Kṛṣṇa *(kṛṣṇa-sevā)*, everything is complete. As confirmed in Caitanya-caritāmṛta (Madhya 22.62), *kṛṣṇe bhakti kaile sarva-karma kṛta haya:* if one is engaged in the devotional service of the Lord, the Supreme Personality of Godhead, everything is automatically accomplished.

This is the śāstra's direction. *yathā taror mūla-niṣecanena tṛpyanti tat-skandha-bhujopaśākhāḥ*. Very practical example. Just like watering, pouring water on the root of the tree, automatically you please the branches, the twigs, the leaves, the flowers, the fruits and everything. Immediately the watering energy is transformed to every part of the tree. It is practical. There is no argument. And another example is given. *prāṇopahārāc ca yathendriyāṇāṁ*. You give food to the stomach, and the energy will be distributed to all the parts of your body. If you want to serve separately, two sweetmeats to the two eyes and two sweetmeats to ears, in this way, it will be simply useless waste of time. Simply one sweetmeat, if you put into the stomach, and immediately you will feel some energy which will be enjoyed by your eyes, by your ears, by your nose, your hands, your legs, your hair, everything. This is the process. So we have manufactured so many types of love except God. This is our defect.

So if you want to broaden your feelings of fellowship to the utmost limit, please try to understand the *Bhagavad-gītā*. You'll get enlightenment; you'll become a real *mahātmā*. You will feel affection even for the cats and dogs and reptiles. In the Seventh Canto of the *Śrīmad-Bhāgavatam* you'll find a statement by Nārada Muni that if there is a snake in your house, you should give it something to eat. Just see how your feelings can expand! You'll care even for a snake, what to speak of other animals and human beings.

So we cannot become enlightened unless we come to the point of understanding God, or Kṛṣṇa. Therefore we are preaching Kṛṣṇa consciousness all over the world. The Kṛṣṇa consciousness movement is not new. As I told you, it is based on the principles of the *Bhagavad-gītā*, and the *Bhagavad-gītā* is an ancient scripture. From the historical point of view it is five thousand years old. And from a prehistorical point of view it is millions of years old. Kṛṣṇa says in the Fourth Chapter, *imaṁ vivasvate yogaṁ proktavān aham avyayam:* "I first spoke this ancient science of yoga to the sun-god." That means Kṛṣṇa first spoke the *Bhagavad-gītā* some millions of years ago. But simply from a historical point of view, *Bhagavad-gītā* has existed since the days of the Battle of Kurukṣetra, which was fought five thousand years ago. So it is older than any other scripture in the world.

Try to understand *Bhagavad-gītā* as it is, without any unnecessary commentary. The words of the *Bhagavad-gītā* are sufficient to give you enlightenment, but unfortunately people have taken advantage of the popularity of the *Bhagavad-gītā* and have tried to express their own philosophy under the shelter of the *Bhagavad-gītā*. That is useless. Try to understand the *Bhagavad-gītā* as it is. Then you will get enlightenment; you will understand that Kṛṣṇa is the center of all activities. And if you become Kṛṣṇa conscious, everything will be perfect and all problems will be solved.

CHAPTER 6

The Secret of Happiness

In the revealed scriptures the Supreme Lord is described as *sac-cid-ānanda-vigraha*. *Sat* means eternal, *cit* means fully cognizant, *ānanda* means joyful, and *vigraha* means that He is a person. Thus the Lord, or the Supreme Godhead, who is one without a second, is a fully cognizant and eternally joyful personality with a full sense of His identity. No one is equal to Him or greater than Him. This is a concise description of the Supreme Lord.

The living entities (*jīvas*) are minute samples of the Supreme Lord, and being so they therefore find in their activities the desire for eternal existence, for complete knowledge, and for happiness. These desires are evident in human society, and in the upper planetary systems (Svargaloka, Janaloka, Tapoloka, Maharloka, Brahmaloka, etc.) the living entities enjoy a longer duration of life, an increased amount of knowledge, and a generally more blissful existence. But even in the highest planet in this material world, where the duration of life and standard of enjoyment are thousands and thousands of times greater than those on earth, there is still old age, disease and death. Consequently the level of enjoyment is insignificant in comparison to the eternal bliss enjoyed in the company of the Supreme Lord. Loving service to the Supreme Lord in different relationships makes even the enjoyment of impersonal *Brahman* as insignificant as a drop of water in comparison to the ocean.

tasyaiva hetoḥ prayateta kovido
na labhyate yad bhramatām upary adhaḥ
tal labhyate duḥkhavad anyataḥ sukhaṁ
kālena sarvatra gabhīra-raṁhasā

(*Śrīmad-Bhāgavatam 1.5.18*)

TRANSLATION

Persons who are actually intelligent and philosophically inclined should endeavor only for that purposeful end which is not obtainable even by wandering from the topmost planet [Brahmaloka] down to the lowest planet [Pātāla]. As far as happiness derived from sense enjoyment is concerned, it can be obtained automatically in course of time, just as in course of time we obtain miseries even though we do not desire them.

PURPORT

Every man everywhere is trying to obtain the greatest amount of sense enjoyment by various endeavors. Some men are busy engaged in trade, industry, economic development, political supremacy, etc., and some of them are engaged in fruitive work to become happy in the next life by attaining higher planets. It is said that on the moon the inhabitants are fit for greater sense enjoyment by drinking *soma-rasa*, and the Pitṛloka is obtained by good charitable work. So there are various programs for sense enjoyment, either during this life or in the life after death. Some are trying to reach the moon or other planets by some mechanical arrangement, for they are very anxious to get into such planets without doing good work. But it is not to happen. By the law of the Supreme, different places are meant for different grades of living beings according to the work they have performed. By good work only, as prescribed in the scriptures, can one obtain birth in a good family, opulence, good education and good bodily features. We see also that even in this life one obtains a good education or money by good work. Similarly, in our next birth we get such desirable positions only by good work. Otherwise, it would not so happen that two persons born in the same place at the same time are seen differently placed according to previous work. But all such material positions are impermanent. The positions in the topmost Brahmaloka and in the lowest Pātāla are also changeable according to our own work. The philosophically inclined person must not be tempted by such changeable positions. He should try to get into the permanent life of bliss and knowledge where he will not be forced to come back again to the miserable material world, either in this or that planet. Miseries and mixed happiness are two features of material life, and they are obtained in Brahmaloka and in other *lokas* also. They are obtained in the life of the demigods and also in the life of the dogs and hogs. The miseries and mixed happiness of all living beings are only of different degree and quality, but no one is free from the miseries of birth, death, old age and disease. Similarly, everyone has his destined happiness also. No one can get more or less of these things simply by personal endeavors. Even if they are obtained, they can be lost again. One should not, therefore, waste time with these flimsy things; one should only endeavor to go back to Godhead. That should be the mission of everyone's life.

Every living being desires the topmost level of enjoyment in this material world, and yet everyone is unhappy here. This unhappiness is present on all the higher planets, despite a longer life span, higher standards of enjoyment and comfort. That is due to the law of material nature. We can increase the duration of life and standard to the highest capacity, and yet by the law of material nature we will be unhappy.

The materialists want to prolong life as much as possible because they have no information of the next life. They want to get the maximum comforts in this present life because they think conclusively that there is no life after death. This ignorance about the eternity of the living being and the change of covering in the material world has played havoc in the structure of modern human society. Consequently there are many problems, multiplied by various plans of modernized man. The plans for solving the problems of society have only aggravated the troubles. Even if it is possible to prolong life more than one hundred years, advancement of human civilization does not necessarily follow. The *Bhāgavatam* says that certain trees live for hundreds and thousands of years. At Vṛndāvana there is a tamarind tree (the place is known as *Imlitala*) which is said to have existed since the time of Lord Kṛṣṇa. In the Calcutta Botanical Garden there is a banyan tree said to be older than five hundred years, and there are many such trees all over the world. Svāmī Śaṅkarācārya lived only thirty-two years, and Lord Caitanya lived forty-eight years. Does it mean that the prolonged lives of the abovementioned trees are more important than Śaṅkara or Caitanya? Prolonged life without spiritual value is not very important.

The reason for this unhappiness is that *the quality of happiness which is suitable for our constitution is different from the happiness which is derived from material activities*. The living entity is a minute particle of the superior spiritual energy of the Lord, which is *sac-cid-ānanda-vigraha*, and therefore he has the necessary propensity for joy which is spiritual in quality. Unfortunately for him, he is trying vainly to attain his enjoyment from the foreign atmosphere of material nature. Our ambition should be aimed at enjoying spiritual bliss and not this temporary happiness.

Hankering after material happiness is called lust, and lusty activities are sure to meet with frustration in the long run. The body of a snake is very cool, but if a man, wanting to enjoy this coolness, garlands himself with a venomous snake, he will surely be killed by the snake's venomous bite. The material senses are compared to snakes; indulgence in material happiness will surely kill our spiritual identity. Therefore a sane man should be ambitious to find the real source of happiness.

In order to find this source, however, we need some knowledge of what that happiness is. There is the story of the foolish man who had no experience with sugar cane. When he asked his friend about the characteristics of sugar cane, he was imperfectly informed that sugar cane resembles the shape of a bamboo stick. Consequently he began trying to extract juice from bamboo sticks, but naturally he was baffled in his attempts. This is the situation with the illusioned living entity who, in his search for eternal happiness, ties to extract happiness from this material world, which is not only full of miseries but is also transient and flickering. In *Bhagavad-gītā* the material world is described as being full of miseries.

ābrahma-bhuvanāl lokāḥ
punar āvartino 'rjuna
mām upetya tu kaunteya
punar janma na vidyate

"From the highest planet in the material world, down to the lowest, all are places of misery, where repeated birth and death take place. But one who attains to My abode, O son of Kuntī, never takes birth again." *(Bhagavad-gītā 8.16)*

The ambition for happiness is natural and good, but the attempt to derive it from inert matter by so-called scientific arrangements is an illusory attempt doomed to frustration. Those who are befooled cannot understand this. How a person is driven by the lust for material happiness is also described in the *Bhagavad-gītā*.

idam adya mayā labdham
imaṁ prāpsye manoratham
idam astīdam api me
bhaviṣyati punar dhanam

"The demoniac person thinks: 'So much wealth do I have today, and I will gain more according to my schemes. So much is mine now, and it will increase in the future, more and more.' " *(Bhagavad-gītā 16.13)*

This atheistic or godless civilization is a huge affair contrived for the gratification of our senses, and now we are all mad after money in order to maintain this empty shell. Money is sought after by everyone because that is the medium of exchange for objects for sense gratification. Obviously the expectation of peace in such an atmosphere of gold rush pandemonium is a utopian dream. As long as there is the slightest tinge of sense gratification or desire for sense gratification, peace will remain far, far away. This is because by nature we are all eternal servants of the Supreme Lord and therefore cannot enjoy anything for our personal interests. It is therefore necessary for us to learn how to employ our senses in the transcendental service of the Lord, and to utilize everything to serve His interest. This alone can bring about much desired peace. A part of the body cannot in itself be independently happy. It can only derive its happiness and pleasure out of serving the entire body. The Supreme Lord is the whole, and we are the parts, but we are all busily engaged in activities of self-interest. No one is prepared to serve the Lord. This is the basic cause for our conditioning in material existence and for our resultant unhappiness.

From the highest executive in his skyscraper office down to the coolie in the street—all are working with the thought of accumulating wealth, legally or illegally. Actually it is all illegal, for to work for one's self-interest is both unlawful and destructive. Even the cultivation of spiritual realization for one's own self-interest is unlawful and destructive. The point is that all activities must be directed to the satisfaction of Kṛṣṇa and His service.

Those who are not engaged in the transcendental loving service of the Supreme Lord wrongfully think that they are accumulating so much money day after day.

āśā-pāśa-śatair baddhāḥ
kāma-krodha-parāyaṇāḥ
īhante kāma-bhogārtham
anyāyenārtha-sañcayān

"Being bound by hundreds and thousands of desires, by lust and anger, they secure money by illegal means for sense gratification." (*Bhagavad-gītā* 16.12)

Consequently, although there is no lack of money in the world, there is a scarcity of peace. So much human energy is being diverted to making money, for the general population has increased its capacity to make more and more dollars, but in the long run the result is that this unrestricted and unlawful monetary inflation has created a bad economy all over the world and has provoked us to manufacture huge and costly weapons to destroy the very result of such cheap money-making. The leaders of the big money-making countries are not really enjoying peace but are making plans to save themselves from imminent destruction by nuclear weapons. In fact, huge sums of money are being thrown into the sea by way of experiments with these dreadful weapons. Such experiments are being carried out not only at huge costs but also at the cost of many lives. In this way the nations are being bound by the laws of *karma*. When men are motivated by the impulse for sense gratification, whatever money is earned is spoiled, being spent for the destruction of the human race. The energy of the human race is thus wasted by the laws of nature because of man's aversion to the Lord, who is actually the proprietor of all energies.

Wealth is worshiped and is referred to as Mother Lakṣmī, or the goddess of fortune. It is her position to serve Lord Nārāyaṇa, the source of all the *naras*, or living beings. The *naras* are also meant to serve Nārāyaṇa under the guidance of the goddess of fortune. The living being cannot enjoy the goddess of fortune without serving Nārāyaṇa, and therefore whoever desires to enjoy her wrongly will be punished by the laws of nature. These laws will make certain that the money itself will bring about destruction instead of peace and prosperity.

Unlawfully accumulated money is now being snatched from miserly citizens by various methods of state taxation for the future civil and international war fund, which is spending money in a wasteful and destructive manner. The citizens are no longer satisfied with just enough money to maintain a family nicely and cultivate spiritual knowledge, both of which are essential in human life. Now everyone wants money unlimitedly to satisfy insatiable desires. In proportion to the people's unlawful desires, their accumulated money is taken away by the agents of illusory energy in the shape of medical practitioners, lawyers, tax collectors, societies, constitutions, so-called holy men, famines, earthquakes, and many similar calamities.

The laws of nature do not allow us to accept more money than is required for proper maintenance. There is ample arrangement by the law of nature to provide every living being with his due share of food and shelter, but the insatiable lusts of human beings have disturbed the arrangement set forth by the Almighty Father of all species of life. By the arrangement of the Supreme Lord, there is an ocean of salt because salt is so necessary for the living being. God has, in the same manner, arranged for sufficient air and light, which are also essential. Anyone can collect any amount of salt from the natural storehouse, but constitutionally we cannot take more salt than what we need. If we take more salt, we spoil the broth, and if we take less salt our food becomes tasteless. On the other hand, if we take only what we require, our food is tasty and we are healthy. Presently there is a great deal of concern over the fact that our natural resources are becoming polluted and exhausted. Actually there is ample supply, but due to misuse and greed everything is being spoiled. What conservationists and ecologists do not understand is that everything will continue to be spoiled by the insatiable lusts of mankind unless this Kṛṣṇa consciousness process is taken up. According to *Śrīmad-Bhāgavatam* , adopting simpler, more natural, and a God-centered lifestyle is the actual method for becoming prosperous:

ime jana-padāḥ svṛddhāḥ
supakvauṣadhi-vīrudhaḥ
vanādri-nady-udanvanto
hy edhante tava vīkṣitaiḥ

TRANSLATION

[Queen Kuntī said:] "All these cities and villages are flourishing in all respects because the herbs and grains are in abundance, the trees are full of fruits, the rivers are flowing, the hills are full of minerals, and the oceans are full of wealth. And this is all due to Your glancing over them." (Śrīmad-Bhāgavatam 1.8.40)

PURPORT

Human prosperity flourishes by natural gifts and not by gigantic industrial enterprises. The gigantic industrial enterprises are products of a godless civilization, and they cause the destruction of the noble aims of human life. The more we increase such troublesome industries to squeeze out the vital energy of the human being, the more there will be dissatisfaction of the people in general, although a select few can live lavishly by exploitation.

The natural gifts such as grains and vegetables, fruits, rivers, the hills of jewels and minerals, and the seas full of pearls are supplied by the order of the Supreme, and as He desires, material nature produces them in abundance or restricts them at times. The natural law is that the human being may take advantage of these godly gifts of nature and thus satisfactorily flourish without being captivated by the exploitative motive of lording it over material nature.

The more we attempt to exploit material nature according to our whims, the more we shall become entrapped by the reaction of such exploitative attempts. If we have sufficient grains, fruits, vegetables, and herbs, then what is the necessity of running a slaughterhouse and killing poor animals?

A man need not kill an animal if he has sufficient grains and vegetables to eat. The flow of river waters fertilizes the fields, and there is more than what we need. Minerals are produced in the hills, and the jewels in the ocean. If the human civilization has sufficient grains, minerals, jewels, water, milk, etc., then why should we hanker after terrible industrial enterprises at the cost of the labor of some unfortunate men? But all these natural gifts are dependent on the mercy of the Lord. What we need, therefore, is to be obedient to the laws of the Lord and achieve the perfection of human life by devotional service. The indications by Kuntī-devī are just to the point. She desires that God's mercy be bestowed upon her and her sons so that natural prosperity will be maintained by His grace.

Kuntī-devī mentions that the grains are abundant, the trees full of fruits, the rivers flowing nicely, the hills full of minerals, and the oceans full of wealth, but she never mentions that industry and slaughterhouses are flourishing, for such things are nonsense that men have developed to create problems.

Now in every city there are slaughterhouses, but does this mean that the slaughterhouses can supply enough so that one can live by eating only meat? No, there will not be an adequate supply. Even meat-eaters have to eat grains, fruits, and vegetables along with their slice of meat. Still, for that daily slice of meat they kill so many poor animals. How sinful this is! If people commit such sinful activities, how can they be happy? This killing should not be done, but because it is being done people are unhappy. However, if one becomes Kṛṣṇa conscious and simply depends on Kṛṣṇa's glance (*tava vīkṣitaiḥ*), Kṛṣṇa will supply everything and there will be no question of scarcity.

Of course, by nature's way the tiger, being a nonvegetarian, does not get food every day. After all, who will face a tiger to become its food? Who will say to the tiger, "Sir, I am an altruist and have come to you to give you food, so take my body"? No one. Therefore the tiger has difficulty finding food. And as soon as the tiger is out, there is an animal that follows it and makes a sound like "fayo, fayo," so that the other animals will know, "Now the tiger is out." So by nature's way the tiger has difficulty. But still Kṛṣṇa supplies it food. After about a week, the tiger will get the chance to catch an animal, and because it does not get fresh food daily, it will keep the carcass in some bush and eat a little at a time. Since the tiger is very powerful, people want to become like a lion or a tiger. But that is not a very good proposition, because if one actually becomes like a tiger one won't get food daily, but will have to search for food with great labor. If one becomes a vegetarian, however, one will get food every day. The food for a vegetarian is available everywhere.

If we depend on God's creation, there will be no scarcity, but simply *ānanda*, bliss. God's creation provides sufficient grains and grass, and while we eat the grains and fruits, the animals like the cows will eat the grass. The bulls will help us produce grains, and they will take only a little, being satisfied with what we throw away. If we take fruit and throw away the skin, the animal will be satisfied with the skin. In this way, with Kṛṣṇa in the center, there can be full cooperation between the trees, animals, human beings, and all living entities. This is Vedic civilization, a civilization of Kṛṣṇa consciousness.

Kuntī-devī prays to the Lord, "This prosperity is due to Your glance." When we sit in the temple of Kṛṣṇa, Kṛṣṇa glances over us, and everything is nice. When sincere souls try to become Kṛṣṇa's devotees, Kṛṣṇa very kindly comes before them in His full opulence and glances upon them, and they become happy and beautiful.

Duḥkha-nivṛtti means avoiding painful situation. So everyone is trying to avoid painful situation. That's a fact. We are struggling. I have got income, say two hundred dollars, so that is not sufficient for me. So I am struggling hard to get five hundred dollars, to avoid this painful situation. Again when in five hundred dollars I feel another pain, so I try for one thousand dollar. In this way go on increasing, and the painful situation will never be mitigated. That will continue. Otherwise, why millionaires are committing suicide? He has got money. But they do not know that any amount of material comforts will not make them happy. That is not possible. So we have repeatedly discussed this fact that other countries...

Like India is advertised very poor country. But still, majority of the people in India, they are happy. People do not know. Although materially they haven't got possession... They have got only two cloth or even one cloth. In the village you will find, they are so poverty-stricken. But still, they are following the Vedic principles, taking bath early in the morning, going to their business, whatever they get, eating, husband, wife, children. They are happy. People say "Primitive." But you want, after all, happiness. Primitive or advanced, what is that? In advanced civilization, if you commit suicide, why not primitive?

People do not know what is actual happiness. Therefore the struggle is going on.

na te viduḥ svārtha-gatiṁ hi viṣṇuṁ
durāśayā ye bahir-artha-māninaḥ
andhā yathāndhair upanīyamānās
te 'pīśa-tantryām uru-dāmni baḍdhāḥ
(Śrīmad-Bhāgavatam 7.5.31)

TRANSLATION

Persons who are strongly entrapped by the consciousness of enjoying material life, and who have therefore accepted as their leader or *guru* a similar blind man attached to external sense objects, cannot understand that the goal of life is to return home, back to Godhead, and engage in the service of Lord Viṣṇu. As blind men guided by another blind man miss the right path and fall into a ditch, materially attached men led by another materially attached man are bound by the ropes of fruitive labor, which are made of very strong cords, and they continue again and again in materialistic life, suffering the threefold miseries.

As stated before, the Supreme Lord is *sac-cid-ānanda-vigraha*, joyful by nature, and therefore He expands Himself by His different energies, parts, and differentiated and plenary portions. The Supreme Lord is the Absolute Truth, and He is one without a second, but He also includes His diverse energies, parts, and plenary portions which are simultaneously one with and different from Him. Because He is joyful by nature, He expands Himself in diverse ways, and the activities of these expansions are called His transcendental pastimes or His *līlā*. These pastimes, however, are not blind and inert; they exhibit full sense, independence, and freedom of action and reaction. The complexities of the actions and the reactions of the diverse energies of the Absolute Truth constitute the subject matter of a vast science called the transcendental science of God, and the *Bhagavad-gītā* is the ABC or primary book of knowledge for students interested in that science. Every intelligent human being should become interested in this transcendental science; indeed, according to the opinions of the sages, human life is only meant for learning this science. The opening words of the *Vedānta-sūtra* proclaim: "Now is the time to inquire about Brahman."

Human life by nature is full of suffering, and lower life forms are even more miserable. Any sane man with properly discriminating senses can understand that life in the material world is full of miseries and that no one is free from the actions and reactions of such miseries. This is not a pessimistic view of life but is an actual fact which we should not be blind to. The miseries of life are divided into three categories, namely miseries arising from the body and mind, miseries arising from other living entities, and miseries arising due to natural calamities. A sane man must look to eliminate these miseries and thereby become happy in life. We are all trying to achieve peace and freedom from these miseries, at least unconsciously, and in the higher intellectual circles there are attempts to get rid of these miseries by ingenious plans and designs. But the power that baffles all the plans and designs of even the most intelligent person is the power of *Māyā devī*, or the illusory energy. The law of *karma*, or the result of all actions and reactions in the material world, is controlled by this all-powerful illusory energy. The activities of this energy function according to principles and regulations, and they act consciously under the direction of the Supreme Lord. Everything is done by nature in full consciousness; nothing is blind or accidental. This material energy is also called Durgā, which indicates that it is a force which is very difficult to surpass. No one can surpass the laws of Durgā by any amount of childish plans.

To get rid of the sufferings of humanity is simultaneously a very difficult and also a very easy affair. As long as the conditioned souls, who are themselves bound up by the laws of nature, manufacture plans to get rid of the three miseries, there will be no solution. The only effective solutions are those mentioned in *Bhagavad-gītā*, and we have to adopt them in our practical lives for our own benefit. The three miseries of material nature are not found in the pastimes of the Supreme Lord. As mentioned before, He is eternally joyful, and His transcendental pastimes are not different from Him. Because He is the Absolute Truth, His name, fame, form, qualities and pastimes are all identical with Him. The pastimes of the Supreme Lord are transcendental to the actual miseries and sufferings of human beings.

The sufferings of humanity are caused by the misuse of the discriminative power or the little independence which is given to individual souls. The fraudulent *swamis* or mental speculators, in order to remain consistent with the theory of monism, must pass off the miseries of mankind as the pastimes of God, but actually these miseries are only the enforced punishments of *Māyā devī* inflicted upon the misguided conditioned souls.

As living entities, we are part and parcel of the Supreme Lord. Indeed, we actually belong to His superior energy. As such, we may join His transcendental pastimes in our unconditioned state of life, but as long as we are conditioned by the laws of *karma*, in contact with the inferior energy, our sufferings are our own creations, born of a gross misuse of our little independence. The impersonalist monists only misguide people by contending that the threefold miseries are a part of the Lord's pastimes. Such impersonalists and monists have misguided their followers because they incorrectly think that the Supreme Lord and the individual souls are equal in all respects. True, the individual souls are equal in quality with the Supreme Lord, but not in quantity. If the individual soul were quantitatively equal to the Supreme Lord, he would have never been subjected to the laws of material nature. Material nature is subordinate to the will of the Supreme Lord, and therefore He cannot be subjected to the laws of material nature. It is contradictory for the Lord to be subjected to the laws of His own inferior energy.

mattaḥ parataraṁ nānyat
kiñcid asti dhanañjaya
mayi sarvam idaṁ protaṁ
sūtre maṇi-gaṇā iva

"O conqueror of wealth (Arjuna), there is no truth superior to Me. Everything rests upon Me, as pearls are strung on a thread." *(Bhagavad-gītā 7.7)*

Again, Śrī Kṛṣṇa states:

tribhir guṇamayair bhāvair
ebhiḥ sarvam idaṁ jagat
mohitaṁ nābhijānāti
mām ebhyaḥ param avyayam

"Deluded by the three modes (goodness, passion, and ignorance), the whole world does not know Me, who am above the modes and inexhaustible." *(Bhagavad-gītā 7.13)*

The individual souls, who are put into the miseries of the material world, are suffering the resultant reactions of their unsanctioned activities. This is the verdict of *Bhagavad-gītā*.

The parts and parcels are meant to serve the whole, and when they misuse their independence they are subject to the miseries of the laws of matter, just as criminals are subject to police action. The state considers its citizens to be its parts and parcels, and when a citizen misuses his relative independence, the state puts him under police authority. The life of a citizen outside the prison and the life of a citizen within the prison are not the same. Similarly, the sufferings of the living entities within the prison of material nature cannot be equated with the pastimes of the Supreme Lord which exist in the absolute freedom of *sac-cid-ānanda*.

No government wants its citizens to act in such a way that they must go to prison and suffer tribulations. The prison house is undoubtedly constructed by the state government, but this does not mean that the government is anxious for its citizens to be put into it. Indirectly, the disobedient citizens force the government to construct the prison house. It is not done for the pleasure of the government, which has to spend a great deal of money in constructing and maintaining it. On the contrary, the government would be very glad to demolish prisons altogether provided that there are no disobedient citizens in the state. In the same way, this material world is created by the Supreme Lord, but the Supreme Lord does not will that living entities be put in it. The living entities themselves make that decision.

Happiness can be attained when you come to God— because you are part and parcel of God. The same example. A little child is crying. Nobody could pacify it. But as soon as the child is put on the breast of the mother, he immediately becomes happy. Because the child is a part and parcel of the mother. And immediately he understands that "Now I have come to safety, my mother." Immediately happy. This is practical. Similarly, we are all part and parcel of God, Visnu. So unless we come to Kṛṣṇa or Viṣṇu— Kṛṣṇa is Viṣṇu there is no happiness. It is not possible. It is not possible. They are trying to become happy by so-called scientific advancement. What is this science? *Atyantika-duhkha-nivrtti.* The aim of life is to come to the platform of happiness, where there is no distress at all, simply happiness. That is our aim. There cannot be any distress. Only happiness. *Anandamayo 'bhyasat.*

So you see so many pictures of Kṛṣṇa. Kṛṣṇa is playing with His cowherd boys; Kṛṣṇa dancing with His girlfriends, *gopis*; Kṛṣṇa is stealing butter; Kṛṣṇa is doing so many—simply happiness, simply happiness. You won't find Kṛṣṇa is morose and sitting or crying. Even if He is killing some demon, very laughingly, as easy job. You see? So either He is killing or dancing, He is happy. So we are giving this information of happiness, the topmost happiness,... *Anandamayo 'bhyasat*. In the *Vedanta-sutra* it is said that spirit soul, the Supersoul or the individual soul, their nature is to become happy. *Anandamaya*. Happy. Spiritual life means happiness. There is no distress. But that happiness can be attained in cooperation with the Supreme. We are sparks of fire. You see sometimes, the sparks; it looks very beautiful. The same spark, as soon as falls down from the fire, extinguished. The fiery quality immediately extinguished. So our material condition is like that. We have given up the company of Kṛṣṇa, and we wanted to be happy in this material world; therefore we are suffering. So same spark, particle of carbon, if you put again to the fire, it will again become red hot and fire. So this is Kṛṣṇa consciousness movement, that we are trying the sparks, which by chance has fallen down from the fire, to pick it up again and put it in the fire. That is real happiness.

In this material world, both the happiness and distress, they are illusion. Illusion. There are many examples. Just like water; in summer season it is happiness, and in winter season it is distress. But the same water. Some water, at one time, it is happiness, and the same water, at one time, it is distress. The same son, when he is born, it is happiness, and the same son, when he's dead, it is distress. But son is the same. So this material world is duality. You cannot understand happiness without distress, and you cannot understand distress without happiness. Therefore it is called relative world. You cannot understand son without understanding a father, and you cannot understand a father without understanding the son. And spiritual happiness is above this duality. Spiritual happiness. So that is the perfection of *yoga*. *Yoga adhyātmikaḥ. Adhyātma, ātmika, atmā*, the soul, the happiness of the soul, that is real *yoga*. The happiness of the soul can be possible when the soul, individual soul, is with the Supersoul, or the Supreme Soul. *Nityo nityānām cetanās cetanānām (Kaṭhā Upaniṣad 2.2.13)*. There is the Supreme Soul, or Supreme Being. There are many living beings. We are many. We living beings, or living entities, we are many. But the principal living being is Kṛṣṇa. The fire and the sparks: the sparks are illuminated when it is with the original fire. If the sparks fall down from the association of the original fire, it is extinguished, no more light. Similarly, our real happiness is when we enjoy with the Supreme Being.

Śrīmad-Bhāgavatam tells how after getting this rare human form of life, one should endeavor for happiness which continues forever:

ṛṣabha uvāca
nāyaṁ deho deha-bhājāṁ nṛloke
kaṣṭān kāmān arhate viḍ-bhujāṁ ye
tapo divyaṁ putrakā yena sattvaṁ
śuddhyed yasmād brahma-saukhyaṁ tv anantam

(*Śrīmad-Bhāgavatam* 5.5.1)

TRANSLATION

Lord Ṛṣabhadeva told His sons: My dear boys, of all the living entities who have accepted material bodies in this world, one who has been awarded this human form should not work hard day and night simply for sense gratification, which is available even for dogs and hogs that eat stool. One should engage in penance and austerity to attain the divine position of devotional service. By such activity, one's heart is purified, and when one attains this position, he attains eternal, blissful life, which is transcendental to material happiness and which continues forever.

PURPORT

In this verse Lord Ṛṣabhadeva tells His sons about the importance of human life. The word *deha-bhāk* refers to anyone who accepts a material body, but the living entity who is awarded the human form must act differently from animals. Animals like dogs and hogs enjoy sense gratification by eating stool. After undergoing severe hardships all day, human beings are trying to enjoy themselves at night by eating, drinking, having sex and sleeping. At the same time, they have to properly defend themselves. However, this is not human civilization. Human life means voluntarily practicing suffering for the advancement of spiritual life. There is, of course, suffering in the lives of animals and plants, which are suffering due to their past misdeeds. However, human beings should voluntarily accept suffering in the form of austerities and penances in order to attain the divine life. After attaining the divine life, one can enjoy happiness eternally. After all, every living entity is trying to enjoy happiness, but as long as one is encaged in the material body, he has to suffer different kinds of misery. A higher sense is present in the human form. We should act according to superior advice in order to attain eternal happiness and go back to Godhead.

It is significant in this verse that the government and the natural guardian, the father, should educate subordinates and raise them to Kṛṣṇa consciousness. Devoid of Kṛṣṇa consciousness, every living being suffers in this cycle of birth and death perpetually. To relieve them from this bondage and enable them to become blissful and happy, *bhakti-yoga* should be taught. A foolish civilization neglects to teach people how to rise to the platform of *bhakti-yoga*. Without Kṛṣṇa consciousness a person is no better than a hog or dog. The instructions of Ṛṣabhadeva are very essential at the present moment. People are being educated and trained to work very hard for sense gratification, and there is no sublime aim in life. A man travels to earn his livelihood, leaving home early in the morning, catching a local train and being packed in a compartment. He has to stand for an hour or two in order to reach his place of business. Then again he takes a bus to get to the office. At the office he works hard from nine to five; then he takes two or three hours to return home. After eating, he has sex and goes to sleep. For all this hardship, his only happiness is a little sex. *Yan maithunādi-gṛhamedhi-sukhaṁ hi tuccham.* Ṛṣabhadeva clearly states that human life is not meant for this kind of existence, which is enjoyed even by dogs and hogs. Indeed, dogs and hogs do not have to work so hard for sex. A human being should try to live in a different way and should not try to imitate dogs and hogs. The alternative is mentioned. Human life is meant for tapasya, austerity and penance. By *tapasya*, one can get out of the material clutches. When one is situated in Kṛṣṇa consciousness, devotional service, his happiness is guaranteed eternally. By taking to *bhakti-yoga*, devotional service, one's existence is purified. The living entity is seeking happiness life after life, but he can make a solution to all his problems simply by practicing *bhakti-yoga.* Then he immediately becomes eligible to return home, back to Godhead. As confirmed in Bhagavad-gītā (4.9):

janma karma ca me divyam
evaṁ yo vetti tattvataḥ
tyaktvā dehaṁ punar janma
naiti mām eti so 'rjuna

"One who knows the transcendental nature of My appearance and activities does not, upon leaving the body, take his birth again in this material world, but attains My eternal abode, O Arjuna."

CHAPTER 7

The Art of Work

buddhi-yukto jahātīha
ubhe sukṛta-duṣkṛte
tasmād yogāya yujyasva
yogaḥ karmasu kauśalam

(*Bhagavad-gītā* 2.50)

TRANSLATION

A man engaged in devotional service rids himself of both good and bad reactions even in this life. Therefore strive for yoga, which is the art of all work.

PURPORT

Since time immemorial each living entity has accumulated the various reactions of his good and bad work. As such, he is continuously ignorant of his real constitutional position. One's ignorance can be removed by the instruction of the *Bhagavad-gītā*, which teaches one to surrender unto Lord Śrī Kṛṣṇa in all respects and become liberated from the chained victimization of action and reaction, birth after birth. Arjuna is therefore advised to act in Kṛṣṇa consciousness, the purifying process of resultant action.

Lord Kṛṣṇa, seeing the distressful condition of the living entities and forseeing their bleak future, spoke the scripture known as *Bhagavad-gītā*, which contains unequivocal instructions for mankind. These instructions are like the cooling showers of peace on the blazing forest fire of material existence. Ordinary human activities are quite different from the activities recommended in the *Śrīmad Bhagavad-gītā*; understanding this difference is essential for us. In our times we find many fruitive workers who claim to be *karma-yogīs* but in fact are seen to enjoy the fruits of their labor. What is needed is not this false *karma-yoga* but genuine *buddhi-yoga*, which Lord Kṛṣṇa several times explains in the *Bhagavad-gītā*. *Buddhi-yoga* means "devotion to the Supreme Lord." The Lord says in the *Bhagavad*-gītā (10.10), "To those who are constantly devoted to serving Me with love, I give the understanding by which they can come to Me." Elsewhere in the *Gītā* (18.56) the Lord says, "One can understand Me as I am, as the Supreme Personality of Godhead, only by devotional service." Therefore, since *buddhi-yoga* is the means to attain the Supreme Lord, then *buddhi-yoga* is nothing other than devotional service. The Supreme Lord is attained through loving devotional service. This fact is well known. Hence the Lord is also known as *bhakta-vatsala*, "He who is especially inclined toward His devotees."

The course of action one chooses through executing *buddhi-yoga* is the very means for mankind to attain lasting peace. Such a course of action will enable man to find rest "in the dispensation of providence." We can clearly understand the essence of *buddhi-yoga* from the *Bhagavad-gītā* (Chapter 2.39-40):

"Thus far I have described this knowledge to you through analytical study. Now listen as I explain it in terms of working without fruitive results. O son of Pṛthā, when you act in such knowledge you can free yourself from the bondage of works. In this endeavor there is no loss or diminution, and a little advancement on this path can protect one from the most dangerous type of fear."

The attainment of peace through the process of *sāṅkhya-yoga* is for the modern man almost impossible. But peace is easily available through the process of *buddhi-yoga*, or loving devotional service to the Supreme Lord. And this peace is of the highest nature: it far exceeds the happiness experienced through any other process. Activities that are directly connected to devotional service blossom and develop unhindered by anything external. The amount of devotional activity one performs always remains intact; it is a permanent spiritual gain for the performer, never to be rendered futile. Even a little execution of devotional service is enough to save one from the greatest type of fear.

The process of pure devotional service is one. At the same, time the *Bhagavad-gītā* points out how to execute *buddhi-yoga* through *jñāna*, or analytical study, and *karma*, or fruitive action. When *buddhi-yoga* is executed in conjunction with fruitive activity, it is known as *karma-yoga*. Similarly, when it is executed in conjunction with analytical study, then it is called *jñāna-yoga*. And when *buddhi-yoga*, or devotional service, transcends both *karma-yoga* and *jñāna-yoga* and becomes completely unalloyed, that devotion is called pure *bhakti-yoga*, or loving devotional service to the Supreme Lord.

The fruitive activities one performs in this world, whether according to social norms or Vedic standards, give different results. Again, by experiencing the fruits of those labors, one creates new sets of activities and their concomitant results, which in turn give rise to newer sets of activities and their results. All these activities and their results cannot automatically be labeled *karma-yoga*. We can see that the process of performing fruitive actions and experiencing their results is like a mammoth tree sprouting endless branches and twigs. Can the performer of actions who experiences the endless fruits of that mammoth tree ever enjoy peace and benediction? No. Therefore it is said, "In the dispensation of providence, mankind cannot have any rest." Even in this lifetime, one who performs fruitive work is totally entangled in the cycle of *karma* as he sits on the tree of material existence. As a result, the soul must enter 8,400,000 species and suffer the threefold miseries, never finding any rest or peace.

Yet people find it impossible to renounce fruitive activities. Even the so-called *sannyāsīs* who make a show of renouncing such activities must still perform many activities, at least to relieve their hunger. Śrīpāda Śaṅkarācārya, seeing the condition of the *sannyāsīs* during his time, commented, "One takes on many different garbs just to fill one's stomach." And trying to give up all activities is no solution. When Śrī Arjuna, a warrior, wanted to forsake his duty of fighting a war, the Supreme Lord, Kṛṣṇa, advised him:

niyataṁ kuru karma tvaṁ
karma jyāyo hy akarmaṇaḥ
śarīra-yātrāpi ca te
na prasiddhyed akarmaṇaḥ

(*Bhagavad-gītā* 3.8)

TRANSLATION

Perform your prescribed duty, for doing so is better than not working. One cannot even maintain one's physical body without work.

PURPORT

There are many pseudo meditators who misrepresent themselves as belonging to high parentage, and great professional men who falsely pose that they have sacrificed everything for the sake of advancement in spiritual life. Lord Kṛṣṇa did not want Arjuna to become a pretender. Rather, the Lord desired that Arjuna perform his prescribed duties as set forth for *kṣatriyas*. Arjuna was a householder and a military general, and therefore it was better for him to remain as such and perform his religious duties as prescribed for the householder *kṣatriya*. Such activities gradually cleanse the heart of a mundane man and free him from material contamination. So-called renunciation for the purpose of maintenance is never approved by the Lord, nor by any religious scripture. After all, one has to maintain one's body and soul together by some work. Work should not be given up capriciously, without purification of materialistic propensities. Anyone who is in the material world is certainly possessed of the impure propensity for lording it over material nature, or, in other words, for sense gratification. Such polluted propensities have to be cleared. Without doing so, through prescribed duties, one should never attempt to become a so-called transcendentalist, renouncing work and living at the cost of others.

A person should never give up his prescribed duty without scriptural authorization, for this will cause chaos in the world. Since it is impossible to maintain the body without activities, it is impossible to totally renounce activities. On the other hand, the tree of material entanglement, which thrives on fruitive activities and their results, can never bring forth any hope for peace. It is for this reason that the Supreme Lord has explained how one is to perform activities:

yajñārthāt karmaṇo 'nyatra
loko 'yaṁ karma-bandhanaḥ
tad-arthaṁ karma kaunteya
mukta-saṅgaḥ samācara

(Bhagavad-gītā 3.9)

TRANSLATION

Work done as a sacrifice for Viṣṇu has to be performed; otherwise work causes bondage in this material world. Therefore, O son of Kuntī, perform your prescribed duties for His satisfaction, and in that way you will always remain free from bondage.

PURPORT

Since one has to work even for the simple maintenance of the body, the prescribed duties for a particular social position and quality are so made that that purpose can be fulfilled. *Yajña* means Lord Viṣṇu, or sacrificial performances. All sacrificial performances also are meant for the satisfaction of Lord Viṣṇu. The Vedas enjoin: *yajño vai viṣṇuḥ*. In other words, the same purpose is served whether one performs prescribed *yajñas* or directly serves Lord Viṣṇu. Kṛṣṇa consciousness is therefore performance of *yajña* as it is prescribed in this verse. The *varṇāśrama* institution also aims at satisfying Lord Viṣṇu. *Varṇāśramācāravatā puruṣeṇa paraḥ pumān/ viṣṇur ārādhyate (Viṣṇu Purāṇa* 3.8.8).

Therefore one has to work for the satisfaction of Viṣṇu. Any other work done in this material world will be a cause of bondage, for both good and evil work have their reactions, and any reaction binds the performer. Therefore, one has to work in Kṛṣṇa consciousness to satisfy Kṛṣṇa (or Viṣṇu); and while performing such activities one is in a liberated stage. This is the great art of doing work, and in the beginning this process requires very expert guidance. One should therefore act very diligently, under the expert guidance of a devotee of Lord Kṛṣṇa, or under the direct instruction of Lord Kṛṣṇa Himself (under whom Arjuna had the opportunity to work). Nothing should be performed for sense gratification, but everything should be done for the satisfaction of Kṛṣṇa. This practice will not only save one from the reaction of work, but also gradually elevate one to transcendental loving service of the Lord, which alone can raise one to the kingdom of God.

It is another kind of "dispensation of providence" when the fruits of actions do not bind one. To perform all activities only as a sacrifice for the satisfaction of Lord Viṣṇu is true freedom from the results of activities, or the real art of *karma-yoga*. Through this process of *karma-yoga* one is freed from the shackles of fruitive results and one's inherent eternal loving devotion for the Supreme Lord gradually manifests. This type of *karma-yoga* is also referred to as desireless actions, or *naiṣkarmya*, or in other words activities performed without expectation of any sense gratification. One who works in this way offers all the results of his actions to the Supreme Lord instead of enjoying them himself.

karmaṇy evādhikāras te
mā phaleṣu kadācana
mā karma-phala-hetur bhūr
mā te saṅgo 'stv akarmaṇi

(Bhagavad-gītā 2.47)

TRANSLATION

You have a right to perform your prescribed duty, but you are not entitled to the fruits of action. Never consider yourself the cause of the results of your activities, and never be attached to not doing your duty.

PURPORT

There are three considerations here: prescribed duties, capricious work, and inaction. Prescribed duties are activities enjoined in terms of one's acquired modes of material nature. Capricious work means actions without the sanction of authority, and inaction means not performing one's prescribed duties. The Lord advised that Arjuna not be inactive, but that he perform his prescribed duty without being attached to the result. One who is attached to the result of his work is also the cause of the action. Thus he is the enjoyer or sufferer of the result of such actions.

As far as prescribed duties are concerned, they can be fitted into three subdivisions, namely routine work, emergency work and desired activities. Routine work performed as an obligation in terms of the scriptural injunctions, without desire for results, is action in the mode of goodness. Work with results becomes the cause of bondage; therefore such work is not auspicious. Everyone has his proprietary right in regard to prescribed duties, but should act without attachment to the result; such disinterested obligatory duties doubtlessly lead one to the path of liberation.

Arjuna was therefore advised by the Lord to fight as a matter of duty without attachment to the result. His nonparticipation in the battle is another side of attachment. Such attachment never leads one to the path of salvation. Any attachment, positive or negative, is cause for bondage. Inaction is sinful. Therefore, fighting as a matter of duty was the only auspicious path of salvation for Arjuna.

All of us must try to earn whatever money is required to maintain ourselves and our family. Money buys food, and food maintains our body. Without sufficient food, the body becomes weak and useless, and then it cannot generate further means for its sustenance. Which is the cause and which the effect is very difficult to establish. Such is the cycle of fruitive activities. Our material existence birth after birth consists of going round the great cycle of fruitive activity. If, by the mercy of the Supreme Lord or His pure representative, a fortunate soul caught in the midst of this turning wheel can understand his distressful condition, he begins to perform activities that will free him from this bondage:

karma-jaṁ buddhi-yuktā hi
phalaṁ tyaktvā manīṣiṇaḥ

janma-bandha-vinirmuktāḥ
padaṁ gacchanty anāmayam

(*Bhagavad-gītā* 2.51)

TRANSLATION

By thus engaging in devotional service to the Lord, great sages or devotees free themselves from the results of work in the material world. In this way they become free from the cycle of birth and death and attain the state beyond all miseries [by going back to Godhead].

PURPORT

The liberated living entities belong to that place where there are no material miseries. The *Bhāgavatam* (10.14.58) says:

samāśritā ye pada-pallava-plavaṁ
mahat-padaṁ puṇya-yaśo murāreḥ
bhavāmbudhir vatsa-padaṁ paraṁ padaṁ
padaṁ padaṁ yad vipadāṁ na teṣām

"For one who has accepted the boat of the lotus feet of the Lord, who is the shelter of the cosmic manifestation and is famous as Mukunda, or the giver of *mukti*, the ocean of the material world is like the water contained in a calf's footprint. *paraṁ padam*, or the place where there are no material miseries, or Vaikuṇṭha, is his goal, not the place where there is danger in every step of life."

Owing to ignorance, one does not know that this material world is a miserable place where there are dangers at every step. Out of ignorance only, less intelligent persons try to adjust to the situation by fruitive activities, thinking that the resultant actions will make them happy. They do not know that no kind of material body anywhere within the universe can give life without miseries. The miseries of life, namely birth, death, old age and diseases, are present everywhere within the material world. But one who understands his real constitutional position as the eternal servitor of the Lord, and thus knows the position of the Personality of Godhead, engages himself in the transcendental loving service of the Lord. Consequently he becomes qualified to enter into the Vaikuṇṭha planets, where there is neither material, miserable life nor the influence of time and death. To know one's constitutional position means to know also the sublime position of the Lord. One who wrongly thinks that the living entity's position and the Lord's position are on the same level is to be understood to be in darkness and therefore unable to engage himself in the devotional service of the Lord. He becomes a lord himself and thus paves the way for the repetition of birth and death. But one who, understanding that his position is to serve, transfers himself to the service of the Lord, at once becomes eligible for Vaikuṇṭhaloka. Service for the cause of the Lord is called *karma-yoga* or *buddhi-yoga*, or in plain words, devotional service to the Lord.

Section IV

Holy Name: The Ultimate Panacea

ajñānād athavā jñānād
uttamaśloka-nāma yat
saṅkīrtitam aghaṁ puṁso
dahed edho yathānalaḥ

(Śrīmad-Bhāgavatam 6.2.18)

TRANSLATION

As a fire burns dry grass to ashes, so the holy name of the Lord, whether chanted knowingly or unknowingly, burns to ashes, without fail, all the reactions of one's sinful activities.

PURPORT

Fire will act, regardless of whether handled by an innocent child or by someone well aware of its power. For example, if a field of straw or dry grass is set afire, either by an elderly man who knows the power of fire or by a child who does not, the grass will be burned to ashes. Similarly, one may or may not know the power of chanting the Hare Kṛṣṇa mantra, but if one chants the holy name he will become free from all sinful reactions.

CHAPTER 8

Sankirtana: The Special Quality in Kali-yuga

The Special Value of Kali-yuga

kaler doṣa-nidhe rājann
asti hy eko mahān guṇaḥ
kīrtanād eva kṛṣṇasya
mukta-saṅgaḥ paraṁ vrajet
(Śrīmad-Bhāgavatam 12.3.51)

TRANSLATION

My dear King, although Kali-yuga is an ocean of faults, there is still one good quality about this age: Simply by chanting the Hare Kṛṣṇa *mahā-mantra*, one can become free from material bondage and be promoted to the transcendental kingdom.

This is a sloka, verse, from *Śrīmad-Bhāgavatam* in connection with conversation with Maharaja Pariksit and Sukadeva Gosvami, and, when the description of this Kali-yuga was given, Maharaja Pariksit became very sorry that, because he was a pious king, he was thinking always of the welfare of the citizens. So when he heard about the description of the Kali-yuga, he was very much disturbed in his mind. Although he was going to die, still he was so compassionate: "Oh, in the age of Kali, the people will suffer so much."

So, when he was so sorry, Sukadeva Gosvami encouraged him, "Maharaja, don't be sorry. There is very nice process in the Kali-yuga. In the midst of so many difficulties of this age, there is one boon, and that boon is one can become liberated from this material entanglement altogether simply by chanting this "*Hare Kṛṣṇa, Hare Kṛṣṇa, Kṛṣṇa Kṛṣṇa, Hare Hare/ Hare Rāma, Hare Rāma, Rāma Rāma Hare Hare*". It was especially mentioned, *kīrtanād eva kṛṣṇasya*, simply by chanting Hare Kṛṣṇa, one can become... This is the greatest boon in this age. The material world is miserable. Just like cold season, this winter season, today we are feeling most inconvenienced. Similarly, this material world is always miserable. But still, in this age it is most miserable, in this age of Kali. But the boon is, the first-class boon is that even there are so many miserable conditions, in the midst of all those disadvantages, one can become free from all contamination simply by Kṛṣṇa..., *kīrtanād eva kṛṣṇasya*. Simply by this.

krte yad dhyayato visnum
tretayam yajato makhaih
dvapare paricaryayam
kalau tad dhari-kirtanat

(Śrīmad-Bhāgavatam 12.3.52)

"Whatever result was obtained in Satya-yuga by meditating on Viṣṇu, in Tretā-yuga by performing sacrifices, and in Dvāpara-yuga by serving the Lord's lotus feet can be obtained in Kali-yuga simply by chanting the Hare Kṛṣṇa *mahā-mantra*."

The *Śrīmad-Bhāgavatam* tells about the essential value of Kali Yuga in the following verse:

kaliṁ sabhājayanty āryā
guṇa jñāḥ sāra-bhāginaḥ

yatra saṅkīrtanenaiva
sarva-svārtho 'bhilabhyate

(Śrīmad-Bhāgavatam 11.5.36)

TRANSLATION

Those who are actually advanced in knowledge are able to appreciate the essential value of this age of Kali. Such enlightened persons worship Kali-yuga because in this fallen age all perfection of life can easily be achieved by the performance of *saṅkīrtana*.

PURPORT

It is stated here that among the four ages—Satya, Tretā, Dvāpara and Kali—Kali-yuga is actually the best because in this age the Lord mercifully distributes the highest perfection of consciousness, namely Kṛṣṇa consciousness, very freely. The word *ārya* has been defined by Śrīla Prabhupāda as "one who is advancing spiritually." The nature of an advanced person is to search for the essence of life. For example, the essence of the material body is not the body itself but the spirit soul that is within the body; therefore an intelligent person gives more attention to the eternal spirit soul than to the temporary body. Similarly, although Kali-yuga is considered to be an ocean of contamination, there is also an ocean of good fortune in Kali-yuga, namely the *saṅkīrtana* movement. In other words, all of the degraded qualities of this age are completely counteracted by the process of chanting the holy names of the Lord. Thus it is stated in the Vedic language,

dhyāyan kṛte yajan yajñais
tretāyāṁ dvāpare 'rcayan
yad āpnoti tad āpnoti
kalau saṅkīrtya keśavam

"Whatever is achieved in Satya-yuga by meditation, in Tretā by offering ritual sacrifices and in Dvāpara by temple worship is achieved in Kali-yuga by chanting the names of Lord Keśava congregationally."

The Vedic process gradually lifts the conditioned entity out of the darkness of *ahaṅkāra*, or false identification with the gross material body, and brings him to the platform of self-realization, or ahaṁ *brahmāsmi*, "I am spirit soul. I am eternal." One has to make further progress to discover that although one is eternal, there is a superior eternal entity, who is the Lord Himself within one's own heart and within every atom in the material universe. Beyond this second phase of self-realization there is the third and final stage of perfection, which is realization of *Bhagavān*, or the Supreme Personality of Godhead, in His own abode.

The Supreme Personality of Godhead is not primarily the superintendent of this world but rather the enjoyer of His own world, which is beyond the most fantastic dreams of the conditioned living entity. In other words, although the king or president of a country is ultimately the controller of the prison department, the king or president derives actual pleasure within his own palace and not in administering justice to the foolish prisoners. Similarly, the Lord appoints the demigods to administer the material creation on His behalf while He Himself personally enjoys the ocean of transcendental bliss in His own transcendental kingdom. Thus, realization of the Lord within His own kingdom is far superior to the primitive understanding that the Lord is the "creator" of the prison of the material world. This realization of *Bhagavān* begins with understanding that there are innumerable Vaikuṇṭha planets in the spiritual sky and that on each of them a particular expansion of Nārāyaṇa dwells with His innumerable devotees who are attached to that particular form. The central and chief planet in the spiritual

sky is called Kṛṣṇaloka, and there the Pe
hibits His supreme and original form of G
Lord Brahmā, *govindam ādi-puruṣaṁ*
Brahmā also states:

īśvaraḥ paramaḥ kṛṣṇaḥ
sac-cid-ānanda-vigrahaḥ
anādir ādir govindaḥ
sarva-kāraṇa-kāraṇam

(Brahma-saṁhitā. 5.1)

Thus, love of Kṛṣṇa and entrance into Kṛṣṇa's planet in the spiritual sky is the most supremely perfect and exalted status of life available anywhere, at any time, throughout the totality of existence. That perfection is available in Kali-yuga simply by chanting the holy names of God: Hare Kṛṣṇa, Hare Kṛṣṇa, Kṛṣṇa Kṛṣṇa, Hare Hare/ Hare Rāma, Hare Rāma, Rāma Rāma, Hare Hare. Therefore every sane man, woman or child should deeply understand the unprecedented opportunity offered by Caitanya Mahāprabhu and seriously take up this chanting process. Only the most unfortunate and irrational person will neglect this transcendental opportunity.

The Most Magnanimous Avatar

The process of chanting the holy names of Krishna—*Hare Kṛṣṇa, Hare Kṛṣṇa, Kṛṣṇa Kṛṣṇa, Hare Hare/ Hare Rāma, Hare Rāma, Rāma Rāma, Hare Hare*—which is very simple, practical and sublime was personally inaugurated by the Supreme Lord Śri Caitanya Mahāprabhu for the deliverance of the people of Kali Yuga. Only five hundred years ago when Western man was directing his exploratory spirit toward studying the physical universe nnavigating the globe, in India Śrī Caitanya was inaugu- and masterminding a revolution directed inward. His move- it swept the subcontinent, gained millions of followers, and rofoundly influenced the future of religious and philosophical thinking, both in India and the West. The Caitanya Caritāmṛta states in this regard:

'pīta'-varṇa dhari' tabe kailā pravartana
prema-bhakti dilā loke lañā bhakta-gaṇa
(Caitanya Caritāmṛta Madhya 20.340)

TRANSLATION

"In the Age of Kali, Lord Kṛṣṇa assumes a golden color and, accompanied by His personal devotees, introduces hari-nāma-saṅkīrtana, the chanting of the Hare Kṛṣṇa mantra. By this process He delivers love for Kṛṣṇa to the general populace."

Śrī Caitanya Mahāprabhu, the golden *avatāra*, appeared in India nearly five hundred years ago. It is the custom in India that when a child is born, an astrologer is called for. When Lord Kṛṣṇa, the Supreme Personality of Godhead, appeared five thousand years ago, Gargamuni was called by His father, and he said, "This child formerly incarnated in three complexions, such as red and golden, and now He has appeared in blackish color." Kṛṣṇa's color is described in the scriptures as blackish, just like the color of a cloud. Lord Caitanya is understood to be Kṛṣṇa appearing in golden complexion.

There is much evidence in Vedic literature that Caitanya Mahāprabhu is an incarnation of Kṛṣṇa, and this is confirmed by scholars and devotees. In the *Śrīmad-Bhāgavatam* it is confirmed that the incarnation of Kṛṣṇa, or God, in this present age, Kali-yuga, will always engage in describing Kṛṣṇa. He is Kṛṣṇa, but as a devotee of Kṛṣṇa He describes Himself. And in this age His bodily complexion will not be blackish. This means that it may be white, it may be red, or it may be yellow, because these four colors—white, red, yellow, and black—are the colors assumed by the incarnations for the different ages. Therefore, since the red, white, and blackish colors were already taken by former incarnations, the remaining color, golden, is assumed by Caitanya Mahāprabhu. His complexion is not blackish, but He is Kṛṣṇa.

Another feature of this *avatāra* is that He is always accompanied by His associates. In the picture of Caitanya Mahāprabhu one will find that He is always followed by many devotees chanting. Whenever God incarnates He has two missions, as stated in the *Bhagavad-gītā*. There Kṛṣṇa says, "Whenever I appear, My mission is to deliver the pious devotees and to annihilate the demons." When Kṛṣṇa appeared, He had to kill many demons. If we see a picture of Viṣṇu we will notice that He has a conchshell, lotus flower, club, and disc. These last two items are meant for killing demons. Within this world there are two classes of men—the demons and the devotees. The devotees are called demigods; they are almost like God because they have godly qualities. Those who are devotees are called godly persons, and those who are nondevotees, atheists, are called demons. So Kṛṣṇa, or God, comes with two missions: to give protection to the devotees and to destroy the demons. In this age Caitanya Mahāprabhu's mission is also like that: to deliver the devotees and to annihilate the nondevotees, the demons. But in this age He has a different weapon. That weapon is not a club or disc or lethal weapon—His weapon is the *saṅkīrtana* movement. He killed the demoniac mentality of the people by introducing the *saṅkīrtana* movement. That is the specific significance of Lord Caitanya. In this age people are already killing themselves. They have discovered atomic weapons with which to kill themselves, so there is no need for God to kill them. But He appeared to kill their demonic mentality. That is possible by this Kṛṣṇa consciousness movement.

dharma pravartana kare vrajendra-nandana
preme gāya nāce loka kare saṅkīrtana

(Caitanya Caritāmṛta Madhya 20.341)

TRANSLATION

"Lord Kṛṣṇa, the son of Nanda Mahārāja, personally introduces the occupational duty of the age of Kali. He personally chants and dances in ecstatic love, and thus the entire world chants congregationally."

The process is that the Lord chants and He dances Himself, and people follow similarly. Just like we are painting the picture: the Lord is dancing and everyone is following. And that following can be continued even up to date. God is always there. It is not that Caitanya is not present here. He's always present, and, whenever there is *saṅkīrtana*, there is this kirtana by the devotees, sincere devotees, it is said that Lord Caitanya is there, present. *Tatra tiṣthami nārada yatra gāyanti mad-bhaktaḥ*. *Suddha-bhakta*, those who are pure devotees. Pure devotee means without any material desire. Those who are pure devotees, those who are determined to go back to Godhead, to Kṛṣṇa, they are called pure devotees. They have lost all interest for any material enjoyment. They are now determined. They are called pure devotees. So this *saṅkīrtana* movement creates pure devotees, who gradually lose all interest in the material enjoyment.

In the *Śrīmad-Bhāgavatam* it is said that this is the incarnation of God in this age. And who worships Him? The process is very simple. Just keep a picture of Lord Caitanya with His associates. Lord Caitanya is in the middle, accompanied by His principal associates—Nityānanda, Advaita, Gadādhara, and Śrīvāsa. One simply has to keep this picture. One can keep it anywhere. It is not that one has to come to us to see this picture. Anyone can have this picture in his home, chant this Hare Kṛṣṇa mantra, and thus worship Lord Caitanya. That is the simple method. But who will capture this simple method? Those who have good brains. Without much bother, if one simply keeps a picture of Śrī Caitanya Mahāprabhu at home and chants Hare Kṛṣṇa, then one will realize God. Anyone can adopt this simple method. There is no expenditure, there is no tax, nor is there any need to build a very big church or temple. Anyone, anywhere, can sit down on the road or beneath a tree and chant the Hare Kṛṣṇa mantra and worship God. Therefore it is a great opportunity. For example, in business or political life one sometimes finds a great opportunity. Those who are intelligent politicians take a good opportunity and make a success of it the first time it comes. Similarly, in this age, those who have sufficient intelligence take to this *saṅkīrtana* movement, and they advance very quickly.

Lord Caitanya is called "the golden *avatāra*." *Avatāra* means "descending, coming down." Just as one may come down from the fifth story or the one-hundredth story of a building, an *avatāra* comes down from the spiritual planets in the spiritual sky. The sky we see with our naked eyes or with a telescope is only the material sky. But beyond this there is another sky, which is not possible to see with our eyes or instruments. That information is in the *Bhagavad-gītā*; it is not imagination. Kṛṣṇa says that beyond the material sky is another sky, the spiritual sky.

We have to take Kṛṣṇa's word as it is. For example, we teach small children that beyond England there are other places, called

Germany, India, etc., and the child has to learn about these places from the version of the teacher because they are beyond his sphere. Similarly, beyond this material sky there is another sky. One cannot experiment to find it, any more than a small child can experiment to find Germany or India. That is not possible. If we want to get knowledge, then we have to accept authority. Similarly, if we want to know what is beyond the material world then we have to accept the Vedic authority, otherwise there is no possibility of knowing. It is beyond material knowledge. One cannot go to the far planets in this universe, what to speak of going beyond this universe. The estimation is that in order to go to the highest planet of this universe with modern machinery one would have to travel for forty thousand light-years. So we cannot even travel within this material sky. Our lifetime and means are so limited that we cannot have proper knowledge of even this material world.

In the *Bhagavad-gītā*, when Arjuna asked Kṛṣṇa, "Will you kindly explain the extent to which Your energies are working?" the Supreme Lord gave him so many instances, and at the end He finally said, "My dear Arjuna, what shall I explain about My energies? It is not actually possible for you to understand. But you can just imagine the expansion of My energies: this material world, which consists of millions of universes, is a display of only one fourth of My creation." We cannot estimate the position of even one universe, and there are millions of universes. Then beyond that is the spiritual sky, and there are millions of spiritual planets. All this information is available from the Vedic literature. If one accepts Vedic literature, then he can get this knowledge. If one doesn't accept it, there is no other means. That is our choice. Therefore, according to Vedic civilization, whenever an *ācārya* speaks he immediately gives references from the Vedic literature. Then others will accept it: "Yes, it is correct." In a law court the lawyer gives references from past judgments of the court, and if his case is tight, the judge accepts. Similarly, if one can give evidence from the Vedas, then it is understood that his position is factual.

This verse from *Srīmad-Bhāgavatam* prophecises the transcendental activities of Lord Caitanya:

kṛṣṇa-varṇaṁ tviṣākṛṣṇaṁ
sāṅgopāṅgāstra-pārṣadam
yajñaiḥ saṅkīrtana-prāyair
yajanti hi su-medhasaḥ

(Śrīmad-Bhāgavatam 11.5.32)

TRANSLATION

In the age of Kali, intelligent persons perform congregational chanting to worship the incarnation of Godhead who constantly sings the names of Kṛṣṇa. Although His complexion is not blackish, He is Kṛṣṇa Himself. He is accompanied by His associates, servants, weapons and confidential companions.

PURPORT

This same verse is quoted by Kṛṣṇadāsa Kavirāja in the *Caitanya-caritāmṛta, Ādi-līlā*, Chapter Three, verse 52. His Divine Grace A.C. Bhaktivedanta Swami Prabhupāda has given the following commentary on this verse. "This text is from *Śrīmad-Bhāgavatam* (11.5.32). Śrīla Jīva Gosvāmī has explained this verse in his commentary on the *Bhāgavatam* known as the *Krama-sandarbha*, wherein he says that Lord Kṛṣṇa also appears with a golden complexion. That golden Lord Kṛṣṇa is Lord Caitanya, who is worshiped by intelligent men in this age. That is confirmed in *Śrīmad-Bhāgavatam* by Garga Muni, who said that although the child Kṛṣṇa was blackish, He also appears in three other colors—red, white and yellow. He exhibited His white and red complexions in the Satya and Tretā ages respectively. He did not exhibit the remaining color, yellow—gold, until He appeared as Lord Caitanya, who is known as Gaurahari.

"Śrīla Jīva Gosvāmī explains that kṛṣṇa-varṇam means Śrī Kṛṣṇa Caitanya. *Kṛṣṇa-varṇam* and Kṛṣṇa Caitanya are equivalent. The name Kṛṣṇa appears with both Lord Kṛṣṇa and Lord Caitanya Kṛṣṇa. Lord Śrī Caitanya Mahāprabhu is the Supreme Personality of Godhead, but He always engages in describing Kṛṣṇa and thus enjoying transcendental bliss by chanting and remembering His name and form. Lord Kṛṣṇa Himself appears as Lord Caitanya to preach the highest gospel. *Varṇayati* means 'utters' or 'describes.' Lord Caitanya always chants the holy name of Kṛṣṇa and describes it also, and because He is Kṛṣṇa Himself, whoever meets Him will automatically chant the holy name of Kṛṣṇa and later describe it to others. He injects one with transcendental Kṛṣṇa consciousness, which merges the chanter in transcendental bliss. In all respects, therefore, He appears before everyone as Kṛṣṇa, either by personality or by sound. Simply by seeing Lord Caitanya one at once remembers Lord Kṛṣṇa. One may therefore accept Him as *viṣṇu-tattva*. In other words, Lord Caitanya is Lord Kṛṣṇa Himself.

"*Sāṅgopāṅgāstra-pārṣadam* further indicates that Lord Caitanya is Lord Kṛṣṇa. His body is always decorated with ornaments of sandalwood and with sandalwood paste. By His superexcellent beauty He subdues all the people of the age. In other descents the Lord sometimes used weapons to defeat the demoniac, but in this age the Lord subdues them with His all-attractive figure as Caitanya Mahāprabhu. Śrīla Jīva Gosvāmī explains that His beauty is His *astra*, or weapon, to subdue the demons. Because He is all-attractive, it is to be understood that all the demigods lived with Him as His companions. His acts were uncommon and His associates wonderful. When He propagated the *saṅkīrtana* movement, He attracted many great scholars and *ācāryas*, especially in Bengal and Orissa. Lord Caitanya is always accompanied by His best associates like Lord Nityānanda, Advaita, Gadādhara and Śrīvāsa.

"Śrīla Jīva Gosvāmī cites a verse from the Vedic literature that says that there is no necessity of performing sacrificial demonstrations or ceremonial functions. He comments that instead of engaging in such external, pompous exhibitions, all people, regardless of caste, color or creed, can assemble together and chant Hare Kṛṣṇa to worship Lord Caitanya. *Kṛṣṇa-varṇaṁ tviṣākṛṣṇam* indicates that prominence should be given to the name Kṛṣṇa. Lord Caitanya taught Kṛṣṇa consciousness and chanted the name of Kṛṣṇa. Therefore, to worship Lord Caitanya, everyone should together chant the *mahā-mantra*—Hare Kṛṣṇa, Hare Kṛṣṇa, Kṛṣṇa Kṛṣṇa, Hare Hare/ Hare Rāma, Hare Rāma, Rāma Rāma, Hare Hare. To propagate worship in churches, temples or mosques is not possible because people have lost interest in that. But anywhere and everywhere, people can chant Hare Kṛṣṇa. Thus worshiping Lord Caitanya, they can perform the highest activity and fulfill the highest religious purpose of satisfying the Supreme Lord.

"Śrīla Sārvabhauma Bhaṭṭācārya, a famous disciple of Lord Caitanya, said: 'The principle of transcendental devotional service having been lost, Śrī Kṛṣṇa Caitanya has appeared to deliver again the process of devotion. He is so kind that He is distributing love of Kṛṣṇa. Everyone should be attracted more and more to His lotus feet, as humming bees are attracted to a lotus flower.'"

The incarnation of Caitanya Mahāprabhu is also described in the *Śrī Viṣṇu-sahasra-nāma,* which appears in Chapter 189 of the *Dāna-dharma-parva of Mahābhārata*. Śrīla Jīva Gosvāmī has quoted this reference as follows*: suvarṇa-varṇo hemāṅgo varāṅ-*

gaś candanāṅgadī. "In His early pastimes He appears as a householder with a golden complexion. His limbs are beautiful, and His body, smeared with the pulp of sandalwood, seems like molten gold." He has also quoted, sannyāsa-kṛc chamaḥ śānto niṣṭhā-śānti-parāyaṇaḥ: "In His later pastimes He accepts the sannyāsa order, and He is equipoised and peaceful. He is the highest abode of peace and devotion, for He silences the impersonalist non devotees."

In the *Śrīmad-Bhāgavatam* there is a list of the *avatāras*, and there is mention of Lord Buddha's name. This *Śrīmad-Bhāgavatam* was written five thousand years ago, and it mentions different names for future times. It says that in the future the Lord would appear as Lord Buddha, his mother's name would be Añjanā, and he would appear in Gayā. So Buddha appeared twenty-six hundred years ago, and the *Śrīmad-Bhāgavatam*, which was written five thousand years ago, mentioned that in the future he would appear. Similarly, there is mention of Lord Caitanya, and similarly the last *avatāra* of this Kali-yuga is also mentioned in the *Bhāgavatam*. It is mentioned that the last incarnation in this age is Kalki. He will appear as the son of a *brāhmaṇa* whose name is Viṣṇu-yaśā, in a place called Śambhala. There is a place in India with that name, so perhaps it is there that the Lord will appear.

So an *avatāra* must conform to the descriptions in the *Upaniṣads*, *Śrīmad-Bhāgavatam*, *Mahābhārata*, and other Vedic literatures. And on the authority of Vedic literature and the commentary of great, stalwart *gosvāmīs* like Jīva Gosvāmī, who was the greatest scholar and philosopher in the world, we can accept Lord Caitanya as an incarnation of Kṛṣṇa.

The Supreme Personality of Godhead, Kṛṣṇa, anxiously desires that all conditioned living entities come back home, back to

Godhead, for an eternal life of bliss and knowledge. Thus, the Lord reveals Himself in each of the four ages—Satya, Tretā, Dvāpara and Kali—in a form appropriate for worship by the human beings of that age. In his *Laghu-bhāgavatāmṛta* (Pūrva-khaṇḍa 1.25), Śrīla Rūpa Gosvāmī states:

kathyate varṇa-nāmābhyāṁ
śuklaḥ satya-yuge hariḥ
raktaḥ śyāmaḥ kramāt kṛṣṇas
tretāyāṁ dvāpare kalau

"The Supreme Lord Hari is described in terms of His color and names as *śukla* [white, or the most pure] in Satya-yuga, and as red, dark blue and black respectively in Tretā, Dvāpara and Kali." Thus, although in each age various names suitable for glorifying the Lord are given, such as Haṁsa and Suparṇa in Satya-yuga, Viṣṇu and Yajña in Tretā-yuga, and Vāsudeva and Saṅkarṣaṇa in Dvāpara-yuga, similar names are not given for Kali-yuga, although such names exist, in order to avoid disclosing cheaply the truth of the incarnation of Śrī Caitanya Mahāprabhu.

In Kali-yuga human society is infested with hypocrisy and superficiality. There is a strong tendency toward imitation and fraud in this age. Therefore the incarnation of Śrī Caitanya Mahāprabhu is revealed in Vedic literature in a confidential, discrete way, so that it will be known to the authorized persons who can then propagate the mission of the Lord on the earth. We actually see in this modern age that many foolish and ordinary persons claim to be God or incarnations, *avatāras*, etc. There are many cheap philosophies and academies that promise, for a moderate fee, to make one God in a short time. Thus, were Caitanya Mahāprabhu's name widely spoken of in Vedic literature, there would soon be a veritable plague of imitation Caitanya Mahāprabhus infesting the world. Therefore, to prevent this pandemonium, discretion is exercised in the Vedic literatures in Kali-yuga, and in a sober, concealed way the actual followers of Vedic culture are informed through the Vedic mantras of the descent of Śrī Caitanya Mahāprabhu. This discrete system, selected by the Lord Himself for His appearance in Kali-yuga, is proving to be greatly successful on the earth planet. And throughout the world millions of people are chanting the holy names of Kṛṣṇa without the unbearable harassment of hundreds and thousands of imitation Caitanya Mahāprabhus. Those who seriously desire to approach the Supreme Personality of Godhead can easily understand the Lord's mission, whereas cynical materialistic rascals, puffed up by false prestige and madly considering their insignificant intelligence to be greater than the intelligence of Lord Kṛṣṇa, cannot understand the beautiful arrangements made by the Lord for His graceful descent into the material world. Thus, although Kṛṣṇa is *śreyasām īśvaraḥ*, or the Lord of all benedictions, such foolish persons turn away from the Lord's mission and in this way deprive themselves of their own true benefit in life.

In Kali-yuga human society is infected with enviousness. There is great envy, even among members of the same family, who constantly quarrel in this age. Similarly, neighbors are envious of each other and of each other's possessions and status. And entire nations, burning with envy, go to war unnecessarily at the risk of genocide caused by terrible modern weapons. But all of these harassments caused by family members, strangers, so-called friends who are unfaithful, opposing nations, financial competition, social disgrace, cancer, etc., can be relieved by taking shelter of the lotus feet of Caitanya Mahāprabhu. It is not possible to save the material body, but one who takes shelter of Caitanya Mahāprabhu loosens the hard knot of the heart that psychologically binds him to the hallucination of identifying with the external body or the subtle material mind. Once this false identification is broken, one can be blissful in any adverse material condition. Those who foolishly try to make the temporary body eternal are wasting their time and neglecting the actual process for making life permanent, which is to take shelter of the lotus feet of Caitanya Mahāprabhu, who is Kṛṣṇa Himself.

Why did Lord Caitanya appear? In the *Bhagavad-gītā* Lord Kṛṣṇa says, "Give up all other engagements and simply engage in My service. I will give you protection from all results of sinful actions." In this material world, in conditional life, we are simply creating sinful reactions. That's all. And because of sinful reactions, we have received this body. If our sinful reactions are stopped we would not have to take a material body; we should get a spiritual body.

What is a spiritual body? A spiritual body is a body which is free from death, birth, disease, and old age. It is an eternal body, full of knowledge and bliss. Different bodies are created by different desires. As long as we have desires for different kinds of enjoyment, we have to accept different kinds of material bodies. Kṛṣṇa, God, is so kind that He awards whatever we want. If we want a tiger's body, with tigerlike strength and teeth with which to capture animals and suck fresh blood, then Kṛṣṇa will give us the opportunity. And if we want the body of a saintly person, a devotee engaged only in the service of the Lord, then He will give us that body. This is stated in the *Bhagavad-gītā*.

If a person engaged in *yoga*, the process of self-realization, somehow or other fails to complete the process, he is given another chance; he is given birth in a family of a pure *brāhmaṇa* or a rich man. If one is fortunate enough to take birth in such a family, he gets all facilities to understand the importance of self-realization. From the very beginning of life our Kṛṣṇa conscious children are getting the opportunity to learn how to chant and dance, so when they are grown up they will not change, but instead will automatically make progress. They are very fortunate. Regardless of whether he is born in America or Europe, a child will advance if his father and mother are devotees. He gets this opportunity. If a child takes birth in a family of devotees, this means that in his last life he had already taken to the *yoga* process, but somehow or other he could not finish it. Therefore the child is given another opportunity to make progress under the care of a good father and mother so that he will again advance. In this way, as soon as one completes his development of God consciousness, then he no longer has to take birth in this material world, but returns to the spiritual world.

Kṛṣṇa says in the *Bhagavad-gītā*: "My dear Arjuna, if one understands My appearance, disappearance, and activities, simply because of this understanding he is given the opportunity to take birth in the spiritual world after giving up this body." One has to give up this body—today, tomorrow, or maybe the day after that. One has to. But a person who has understood Kṛṣṇa will not have to take another material body. He goes directly to the spiritual world and takes birth in one of the spiritual planets. So Kṛṣṇa says that as soon as one gets this body—it doesn't matter if it is from India or the moon or the sun or Brahmaloka or anywhere within this material world—one should know that it is due to his sinful activities. There are degrees of sinful activities, so according to the degree of sinfulness, one takes a material body. Therefore our real problem is not how to eat, sleep, mate, and defend—our real problem is how to get a body that is not material but spiritual. That is the ultimate solution to all problems. So Kṛṣṇa guarantees that if one surrenders unto Him, if one becomes fully Kṛṣṇa conscious, then He will give one protection from all reactions to sinful life.

Caitanya Mahāprabhu gives us the opportunity to reach God directly. When Rūpa Gosvāmī, the principal disciple of Lord Caitanya, first saw Caitanya Mahāprabhu, he was a minister in the government of Bengal but wanted to join Caitanya Mahāprabhu's movement. So he gave up his position as a minister, and after joining, when he surrendered, he offered a nice prayer to Lord Caitanya. This prayer says:

namo mahā-vadānyāya
kṛṣṇa-prema-pradāya te
kṛṣṇāya kṛṣṇa-caitanya-
nāmne gaura-tviṣe namaḥ

(Caitanya caritāmṛta, Madhya 19.53)

"My dear Lord, You are the most munificent of all the incarnations." Why? *Kṛṣṇa-prema-pradāya te*: "You are directly giving love of God. You have no other purpose. Your process is so nice that one can immediately learn to love God. Therefore You are the most munificent of all incarnations. And it is not possible for any personality other than Kṛṣṇa Himself to deliver this benediction; therefore I say that You are Kṛṣṇa." *Kṛṣṇāya kṛṣṇa-caitanya-nāmne*: "You are Kṛṣṇa, but You have assumed the name Kṛṣṇa Caitanya. I surrender unto You."

So this is the process. Caitanya Mahāprabhu is Kṛṣṇa Himself, and He is teaching how to develop love of God by a very simple method. He says simply to chant Hare Kṛṣṇa.

harer nāma harer nāma
harer nāmaiva kevalam
kalau nāsty eva nāsty eva
nāsty eva gatir anyathā

(Caitanya caritāmṛta, Ādi 17.21)

"In this age, simply go on chanting the Hare Kṛṣṇa mantra. There is no other alternative." People are embarrassed by so many methods of realization. They cannot take to the actual ritualistic processes of meditation or *yoga*; it is not possible. Therefore Lord Caitanya says that if one takes up this process of chanting, then immediately he can reach the platform of realization.

The chanting process offered by Lord Caitanya for achieving love of God is called *saṅkīrtana*. *Saṅkīrtana* is a Sanskrit word. *Sam* means *samyak*—"complete." And *kīrtana* means "glorifying" or "describing." So complete description means complete glorification of the Supreme, or the Supreme Complete Whole. It is not that one can describe anything or glorify anything and that will be *kīrtana*. From the grammatical point of view that may be *kīrtana*, but according to the Vedic system, *kīrtana* means describing the supreme authority, the Absolute Truth, the Supreme Personality of Godhead. That is called *kīrtana*.

Śrīmad-Bhāgavatam further glorifies Lord Caitanya's *saṇkīrtana* movement:

na hy ataḥ paramo lābho
dehināṁ bhrāmyatām iha
yato vindeta paramāṁ
śāntiṁ naśyati saṁsṛtiḥ

(*Śrīmad-Bhāgavatam* 11.5.37)

TRANSLATION

Indeed, there is no higher possible gain for embodied souls forced to wander throughout the material world than the Supreme Lord's *saṅkīrtana* movement, by which one can attain the supreme peace and free oneself from the cycle of repeated birth and death.

PURPORT

In the *Skanda Purāṇa*, as well as in other *Purāṇas,* there is the following statement: *mahā-bhāgavatā nityaṁ kalau kurvanti kīrtanam.* "During Kali-yuga the great devotees of the Lord always engage in *kīrtana,* chanting the Lord's holy names." It is the nature of the Supreme Personality of Godhead to be merciful, and He is especially merciful to those who, in a helpless condition, take complete shelter of His lotus feet. One can immediately take shelter of the lotus feet of the Lord by chanting His holy names. According to Śrīdhara Svāmī, even in previous ages such as Satya-yuga it was not possible for the living entities to achieve the perfection that is available in Kali-yuga. Śrīla Jīva Gosvāmī has explained this as follows. In former ages such as Satya-yuga human beings were perfectly qualified and easily performed even the most difficult spiritual processes, meditating for many thousands of years practically without eating or sleeping. Thus, although in any age one who completely takes shelter of the Lord's holy name gets all perfection, the highly qualified inhabitants of Satya-yuga do not consider that merely moving the tongue and lips, chanting the Lord's holy name, is a complete process and that the Lord's holy name is the only shelter within the universe. They are more attracted to the difficult and elaborate *yoga* system of meditation, complete with sophisticated sitting postures, painstaking control of the breath and deep, extended meditations in trance on the Personality of Godhead within the heart. In Satya-yuga sinful life is practically unheard of, and therefore people are not afflicted with the terrible reactions seen in Kali-yuga, such as world war, famine, plague, drought, insanity, etc. Although in Satya-yuga people always worship the Personality of Godhead as the ultimate goal of life and meticulously follow His laws, called *dharma*, they do not feel themselves to be in a helpless condition, and thus they do not always experience intense love for the Lord.

However, in Kali-yuga living conditions are so unbearable, modern governments are so obnoxious, our bodies are so ridden by physical and mental disease, and even self-preservation is so troublesome, that the conditioned souls intensely cry out the holy name of Kṛṣṇa, begging for relief from the onslaught of this age. The members of the Kṛṣṇa consciousness movement have vivid and unforgettable experiences of the terrible contradictions inherent in human society in this age, and thus they are firmly convinced that there is nothing to be achieved except the mercy of the Supreme Lord. In ISKCON centers throughout the world we observe wonderfully ecstatic *kīrtana* performances in which men, women and children from all walks of life chant with startling enthusiasm the holy names of Kṛṣṇa and dance in ecstasy, becoming completely indifferent to so-called public opinion. In America a prominent professor from Oberlin College visited a Hare Kṛṣṇa center in California and was astonished by the enthusiasm with which the devotees chant the holy name of Kṛṣṇa in their congregational performances.

Thus, due to their helpless and pathetic condition, the living entities in Kali-yuga have great impetus to surrender fully to the holy name of Kṛṣṇa, putting all of their hope and faith in the Lord's holy name. Kali-yuga is therefore the best age because in this age, more than in Satya-yuga or other ages, the conditioned souls become disgusted with the kingdom of illusion and surrender fully to the Lord's holy name. This status of full surrender is called *paramāṁ śāntim*, or supreme peace.

Śrīla Madhvācārya has quoted a passage from the book called *Svābhāvya* to the effect that a bona fide spiritual master in disciplic succession is able to understand the mentality and capability of his disciples and engage them in worshiping the particular form of the Lord suitable for them. In this way the spiritual master destroys all obstacles in the path of his disciples. The general rule is that one must worship the particular form of the Lord that appears in the current *yuga*. One may also offer his love and worship to other forms of the Lord that appear in other ages, and specifically one is recommended to chant the holy names of Lord Nṛsiṁhadeva to get all protection. Practically all of these injunctions are being carried out within the ISKCON movement. Within the Kṛṣṇa consciousness society, men, women and children are all being engaged in worshiping the Lord according to their particular natures. In addition, according to Caitanya Mahāprabhu's order, we are worshiping Balarāma and Kṛṣṇa, who appeared in Dvāpara-yuga, because They are the original Supreme Personality of Godhead. Similarly, by chanting the Daśāvatāra-stotra, jaya jagadīśa hare, and by reading *Śrīmad-Bhāgavatam*, the members of ISKCON worship all of the plenary expansions of the Personality of Godhead. And after every *ārati* performance devotional prayers are duly chanted to Lord Nṛsiṁhadeva for protection of this movement, which is so essential to human society.

What is the problem of our lives? That we do not know. Modern education never gives enlightenment about the real problem of life. That is indicated in the *Bhagavad-gītā*. Those who are educated and are advancing in knowledge should know what is the problem of life. This problem is stated in the *Bhagavad-gītā*: one should always see the inconveniences of birth, death, old age, and disease. Unfortunately no one pays attention to these problems. When a man is diseased he thinks, "All right. Let me go to the doctor. He will give me some medicine, and I will be cured." But he does not consider the problem very seriously. "I did not want this disease. Why is there disease? Is it not possible to become free from disease?" He never thinks that way. This is because his intelligence is very low-grade, just like that of an animal. An animal suffers, but it has no sense. If an animal is brought to a slaughterhouse and sees that the animal before him is being slaughtered, he will still stand there contentedly eating the grass. This is animal life. He does not know that next time it will be his turn and he will be slaughtered.

Similarly, Mahārāja Yudhiṣṭhira was asked by Yamarāja, "What is the most wonderful thing in this world? Can you explain?" So Mahārāja Yudhiṣṭhira answered, "Yes. The most wonderful thing is that at every moment one can see that his friends, his fathers, and his relatives have died, but he is thinking, 'I shall live forever.'" He never thinks that he will die, just as an animal never thinks that at the next moment he may be slaughtered. He is satisfied with the grass, that's all. He is satisfied with the sense gratification. He does not know that he is also going to die.

My father has died, my mother has died, he has died, she has died. So I will also have to die. Then what is after death? I do not know. This is the problem. People do not take this problem seriously, but the *Bhagavad-gītā* indicates that that is real education. Real education is to inquire why, although we do not want to die, death comes. That is real inquiry. We do not want to become old men. Why does old age come upon us? We have many problems, but this is the sum and substance of all of them.

In order to solve this problem, Lord Caitanya Mahāprabhu prescribes the chanting of Hare Kṛṣṇa. As soon as our heart is cleansed by chanting this Hare Kṛṣṇa mantra, the blazing fire of our problematic material existence is extinguished. How is it extinguished? When we cleanse our heart we will realize that we do not belong to this material world. Because people are identifying with this material world, they are thinking, "I am an Indian, I am an Englishman, I am this, I am that." But if one chants the Hare Kṛṣṇa mantra, he will realize that he is not this material body. "I do not belong to this material body or this material world. I am a spirit soul, part and parcel of the Supreme. I am eternally related with Him, and I have nothing to do with the material world." This is called liberation, knowledge. If I don't have anything to do with this material world, then I am liberated. And that knowledge is called *brahma-bhūta*.

Introduction to Maha-Mantra

The transcendental vibration established by the chanting of Hare Kṛṣṇa, Hare Kṛṣṇa, Kṛṣṇa Kṛṣṇa, Hare Hare/ Hare Rāma, Hare Rāma, Rāma Rāma, Hare Hare is the sublime method for reviving our transcendental consciousness. As living spiritual souls, we are all originally Kṛṣṇa conscious entities, but due to our association with matter from time immemorial, our consciousness is now adulterated by the material atmosphere. The material atmosphere, in which we are now living, is called *māyā*, or illusion. *Māyā* means "that which is not." And what is this illusion? The illusion is that we are all trying to be lords of material nature, while actually we are under the grip of her stringent laws. When a servant artificially tries to imitate the all-powerful master, he is said to be in illusion. We are trying to exploit the resources of material nature, but actually we are becoming more and more entangled in her complexities. Therefore, although we are engaged in a hard struggle to conquer nature, we are ever more dependent on her. This illusory struggle against material nature can be stopped at once by revival of our eternal Kṛṣṇa consciousness. Hare Kṛṣṇa, Hare Kṛṣṇa, Kṛṣṇa Kṛṣṇa, Hare Hare is the transcendental process for reviving this original, pure consciousness. By chanting this transcendental vibration, we can cleanse away all misgivings within our hearts. The basic principle of all such misgivings is the false consciousness that I am the lord of all I survey.

Kṛṣṇa consciousness is not an artificial imposition on the mind. This consciousness is the original, natural energy of the living entity. When we hear this transcendental vibration, this consciousness is revived. This simplest method of meditation is recommended for this age. By practical experience also, one can perceive that by chanting this *mahā-mantra*, or the Great Chanting for Deliverance, one can at once feel a transcendental ecstasy coming through from the spiritual stratum. In the material concept of life we are busy in the matter of sense gratification, as if we were in the lower, animal stage. A little elevated from this status of sense gratification, one is engaged in mental speculation for the purpose of getting out of the material clutches. A little elevated from this speculative status, when one is intelligent enough, one tries to find out the supreme cause of all causes—within and without. And when one is factually on the plane of spiritual understanding, surpassing the stages of sense, mind, and intelligence, he is then on the transcendental plane. This chanting of the Hare Kṛṣṇa mantra is enacted from the spiritual platform, and thus this sound vibration surpasses all lower strata of consciousness—namely sensual, mental, and intellectual. There is no need, therefore, to understand the language of the mantra, nor is there any need for mental speculation nor any intellectual adjustment for chanting this *mahā-mantra*. It is automatic, from the spiritual platform, and as such, anyone can take part in the chanting without any previous qualification. In a more advanced stage, of course, one is not expected to commit offenses on the grounds of spiritual understanding.

Hare Kṛṣṇa, Hare Kṛṣṇa, Kṛṣṇa Kṛṣṇa, Hare Hare/ Hare Rāma, Hare Rāma, Rāma Rāma, Hare Hare. Now, this sound is transcendental sound, sound incarnation of the Absolute Truth. Just try to understand what is incarnation. Incarnation means... The Sanskrit word is *avatāra*, and that is translated into English as "incarnation." The root meaning of *avatāra* is "which comes from the transcendental sky, the spiritual sky to the material sky." That is called *avatāra*. *Avatāraṇa*. Just like... *Avatāraṇa* means "coming from up to down." That is called *avatāraṇa*. And *avatāra* is understood that when God or His bona fide representative comes from that sky to this material plane, that is called *avatāra*.

There is no doubt that chanting for a while takes one immediately to the spiritual platform, and one shows the first symptom of this in the urge to dance along with the chanting of the *mantra*. We have seen this practically. Even a child can take part in the chanting and dancing. Of course, for one who is too entangled in material life, it takes a little more time to come to the standard point, but even such a materially engrossed man is raised to the spiritual platform very quickly. When the *mantra* is chanted by a pure devotee of the Lord in love, it has the greatest efficacy on hearers, and as such this chanting should be heard from the lips of a pure devotee of the Lord, so that immediate effects can be achieved. As far as possible, chanting from the lips of nondevotees should be avoided. Milk touched by the lips of a serpent has poisonous effects.

The word *Harā* is the form of addressing the energy of the Lord, and the words Kṛṣṇa and Rāma are forms of addressing the Lord Himself. Both Kṛṣṇa and Rāma mean "the supreme pleasure," and *Harā* is the supreme pleasure energy of the Lord, changed to *Hare* in the vocative. The supreme pleasure energy of the Lord helps us to reach the Lord.

The material energy, called *māyā*, is also one of the multi-energies of the Lord. And we, the living entities, are also the energy, marginal energy, of the Lord. The living entities are described as superior to material energy. When the superior energy is in contact with the inferior energy, an incompatible situation arises; but when the superior marginal energy is in contact with the superior energy, *Harā*, it is established in its happy, normal condition.

These three words, namely Hare, Kṛṣṇa, and Rāma, are the transcendental seeds of the *mahā-mantra*. The chanting is a spiritual call for the Lord and His energy, to give protection to the conditioned soul. This chanting is exactly like the genuine cry of a child for its mother's presence. Mother *Harā* helps the devotee achieve the Lord Father's grace, and the Lord reveals Himself to the devotee who chants this mantra sincerely. No other means of spiritual realization is as effective in this age of quarrel and hypocrisy as the chanting of the *mahā-mantra*: Hare Kṛṣṇa, Hare Kṛṣṇa, Kṛṣṇa Kṛṣṇa, Hare Hare/ Hare Rāma, Hare Rāma, Rāma Rāma, Hare Hare.

So this sound, this Hare Kṛṣṇa, Hare Kṛṣṇa, Kṛṣṇa Kṛṣṇa, Hare Hare/ Hare Rāma, Hare Rāma, Rāma Rāma, Hare Hare, is the sound representation of the Supreme Lord. *sarvaṁ khalv idaṁ brahma.* The whole thing, either material or spiritual, whatever we have got experience, nothing is separated from the Supreme Absolute Truth. Nothing is separated. Everything has emanated from the Absolute Truth. The example... Just like earth. Earth, then from earth, you have got wood, fuel. From fuel, when you get fire, first of all there is smoke. Then, after smoke, there is fire. And from fire, you can take work. Now, beginning from earth, from earth there is wood; from wood there is smoke; from smoke there is fire. There is a link between the fire and the earth. But the work of the fire, the benefit of the fire, can be had at the last stage, when there is real ignition of fire. Similarly, there is link. The whole material cosmic situation, manifestation, what we see, it is just like the smoke. The fire is behind it. That is spiritual sky. But still, in the smoke, you can feel some heat also. So similarly, this sound vibration of the spiritual world is here so that even in this material world, where there is a scarcity of that spiritual fire, we can appreciate, we can feel, the warmth of that fire.

This transcendental sound vibration is the tool to respiritualize our mind and senses, just like the example of an iron rod. Iron rod, you put into the fire. It gets warm—warm, warmer, warmer. And when it is red hot, then it is no longer iron. Iron it is, but it does not act as iron, but it acts as fire. That iron rod which is red hot in association with fire, you can take that rod and touch anything; it will burn. That means it is no longer acting as iron; it is acting as fire. Similarly, if you associate with this transcendental incarnation, sound incarnation of God, then you will be gradually godly. You will be godly. You can become godly with God's association, not by any other material, extraneous things. No. Just like you can have fire only in association with fire, not with water. If you want to get yourself warm, then you have to associate with fire, not with water, not with air. Similarly, if you want to spiritualize your vision, if you want to spiritualize your action, if you want to spiritualize the whole constitution of your existence, then you have to associate with the supreme spirit. And that supreme spirit is very kind because He is everything. That we have already explained. Everything is interrelated with the Supreme; therefore He is interrelated with sound also. So by God's inconceivable potency, He can present before yourself in sound incarnation. That is His potency. He can do that. And therefore between this name, Kṛṣṇa, and the Supreme Lord Kṛṣṇa, there is no difference.

Bhakti-rasāmṛta-sindhu (1.2.234), states in this regard:

ataḥ śrī-kṛṣṇa-nāmādi
na bhaved grāhyam indriyaiḥ

sevonmukhe hi jihvādau
svayam eva sphuraty adaḥ

TRANSLATION

"Therefore material senses cannot appreciate Kṛṣṇa's holy name, form, qualities and pastimes. When a conditioned soul is awakened to Kṛṣṇa consciousness and renders service by using his tongue to chant the Lord's holy name and taste the remnants of the Lord's food, the tongue is purified, and one gradually comes to understand who Kṛṣṇa really is."

So Lord Kṛṣṇa, Lord Caitanya, He introduced this Hare Kṛṣṇa, Hare Kṛṣṇa, Kṛṣṇa Kṛṣṇa, Hare Hare/ Hare Rāma, Hare Rāma, Rāma Rāma, Hare Hare for this age. And He recommended, *kalau nāsty eva nāsty eva...* Not recommended by His own brain, but it is recommended in the scriptures:

harer nāma harer nāma
harer nāmaiva kevalam
kalau nāsty eva nāsty eva
nāsty eva gatir anyathā

(*Bṛhan-nāradīya Purāṇa* 3.8.126)

TRANSLATION

'In this Age of Kali there is no other means, no other means, no other means for self-realization than chanting the holy name, chanting the holy name, chanting the holy name of Lord Hari.'

In this age, almost no one can perform all the difficult ritualistic ceremonies for becoming liberated. Therefore all the *śāstras* and all the *ācāryas* have recommended that in this age one simply chant the holy name. That will bring one all perfection.

If you want to realize the Supreme Truth, then you must realize this: Hare Kṛṣṇa, Hare Kṛṣṇa, Kṛṣṇa Kṛṣṇa, Hare Hare/ Hare Rāma, Hare Rāma, Rāma Rāma, Hare Hare. *harer nāma harer nāmaharer nāmaiva kevalam:* "Only this." And if you think, "Oh, only this? Why not other?" No. *kalau nāsty eva nāsty eva nāsty eva gatir anyathā. Nāsty eva* means "There is no alternative." And He repeats this: "no alternative, no alternative, no alternative," three times. Three times. That means He is giving too much stress. So our process is like that, that we are following a great personality, Lord Sri Caitanya Mahaprabhu. He introduced from the scripture, not in His own way. Nothing should be accepted which is not recognized. So this is recognized method. Now it depends on us. Let us follow this process and see how we are making progress in the spiritual path.

CHAPTER 9

The Benefits of Chanting

Various Benefits of Chanting

Everyone knows that a happy life requires good health. Proper diet, adequate exercise, and sufficient rest are necessary to keep our bodies strong and fit. If we neglect these demands, our bodies become weakened and resistance wanes. Highly susceptible to infection, we eventually become ill.

More important, but less well known, is the inner self's need for spiritual nourishment and attention. If we ignore our spiritual health requirements, we become overwhelmed by negative material tendencies like anxiety, hatred, loneliness, prejudice, greed, boredom, envy, and anger.

In order to counteract and prevent these subtle infections of the self, we should, as recommended in the Vedic literatures, incorporate into our lives a program of self-examination and steady inner growth, based on spiritual strength and clarity of thought.

The transcendental potency necessary for developing complete psychological and spiritual fulfillment is already present within everyone. It must, however, be uncovered by a genuine spiritual process. Of all such authentic processes, India's timeless *Vedas* tell us that meditation on the Hare Kṛṣṇa mantra is the most powerful.

The initial result of chanting the Hare Kṛṣṇa *mantra* is summarized by Śrīla Prabhupāda in his commentary on the *Bhagavad-gītā:* "We have practical experience that any person who is chanting the holy names of Kṛṣṇa (Hare Kṛṣṇa, Hare Kṛṣṇa, Kṛṣṇa Kṛṣṇa, Hare Hare/ Hare Rāma, Hare Rāma, Rāma Rāma, Hare Hare) in course of time feels some transcendental pleasure and very quickly becomes purified of all material contamination."

In the preliminary stages of chanting, the practitioner experiences a clearing of consciousness, peace of mind, and relief from unwanted drives and habits. As one develops more realization by chanting, he perceives the original, spiritual existence of the self. According to the *Bhagavad-gītā,* this enlightened state "is characterized by one's ability to see the self by the pure mind and to relish and rejoice in the self."

And in the *Caitanya-caritāmṛta,* a seventeen-volume commentary on the life and teachings of Śrī Caitanya, founder of the modern-day Kṛṣṇa consciousness movement, the ultimate benefit of chanting is described. "The result of chanting is that one awakens his love for Kṛṣṇa and tastes transcendental bliss. Ultimately, one attains the association of Kṛṣṇa and engages in His devotional service, as if immersing himself in a great ocean of love."

So by chanting Hare Kṛṣṇa, one reaps innumerable benefits, culminating in Kṛṣṇa consciousness and love of God. We can realize the fruits of chanting by adopting the process of *mantra* meditation and applying it systematically. For clear understanding of the progressive effects of chanting, some of the more important benefits are discussed separately.

Peace of Mind

Initially meditation focuses on controlling the mind, for in our normal condition, we are slaves to any whimsical thoughts, desires, and appetites the mind may generate. We think of something and immediately we want to do it. But the *Bhagavad-gītā* tells us that the meditator must learn to control the mind: "For one who has conquered the mind, then his mind is the best of friends; but for one who has failed to do so, his mind will be the greatest enemy."

The materialistic mind attempts to enjoy by employing the senses to experience matter and material relationships. It is full of unlimited ideas for sense gratification, and being perpetually restless, it constantly flickers from one sense object to another. In doing so, the mind vacillates between hankering for some material gain and lamenting some loss or frustration.

In the *Bhagavad-gītā* Kṛṣṇa explains, "One who is not in transcendental consciousness can have neither a controlled mind nor steady intelligence, without which there is no possibility of peace. And how can there be any happiness without peace?" By chanting the Hare Kṛṣṇa mantra, we can control the mind, instead of letting it control us.

Mantra is a Sanskrit word. *Man* means "mind," and *tra* means "to deliver." Thus, a *mantra* is a transcendental sound vibration with potency to liberate the mind from material conditioning.

In his commentary on *Śrīmad-Bhāgavatam*, Śrīla Prabhupāda explains, "Our entanglement in material affairs is begun from material sound." Each day we hear material sounds from radio and television, from friends and relatives, and based on what we hear, we act. But as Śrīla Prabhupāda points out, "There is sound in the spiritual world also. If we approach that sound, then our spiritual life begins." When we control the mind by focusing it on the purely spiritual sound vibration of the Hare Kṛṣṇa *mantra,* the mind becomes calm. As "music has charms to soothe a savage beast," so the spiritual sound of the *mantra* soothes the restless mind. The Hare Kṛṣṇa *mantra,* being imbued with God's own supreme energies, has the power to subdue all kinds of mental disturbance. Just as a reservoir of water is transparent when unagitated, our mental perceptions become clear and pure when the mind is no longer agitated by the waves of material desires. The mind in its pure state, like a mirror cleansed of dust, will then reflect undistorted images of reality, allowing us to go beneath the surface and perceive the essential spiritual quality of all life's experiences.

Knowledge of the Self

The *Vedas* state that consciousness is a symptom of the soul. In its pure condition, the soul exists in the spiritual world; but when it falls down into contact with matter, the living being is covered by an illusion called false egoism. False ego bewilders the consciousness, causing us to identify with our material bodies. But we are not our material body. When we look at our hand or leg, we say, "This is my hand" or "This is my leg." The conscious self, the "I," is therefore the owner and observer of the body. Intellectually, this fact is easily understandable, and by the spiritual realization that results from chanting, this truth can be directly and continuously experienced.

When the living being identifies with the material body and loses awareness of his real, spiritual self, he inevitably fears death, old age, and disease. He fears loss of beauty, intelligence, and strength and experiences countless other anxieties and false emotions relating to the temporary body. But by chanting, even in the early stages, we realize ourselves to be pure and changeless spirit souls, completely distinct from the material body. Because the *mantra* is a completely pure spiritual sound vibration, it has the power to restore our consciousness to its original, uncontaminated condition. At this point, we cease to be controlled by jealousy, bigotry, pride, envy, and hatred. As Lord Kṛṣṇa tells us in *Bhagavad-gītā,* the soul is "unborn, eternal, ever-existing, undying, and primeval." As our false bodily identification dissolves and we perceive our true transcendental existence, we automatically transcend all the fears and anxieties of material existence. We no longer think "I am American. I am Russian. I am black. I am white."

Attaining real self-awareness also gives us the ability to see the spiritual nature of all living beings. When our natural, spiritual feelings are awakened, we experience the ultimate unity of all life. This is what it means to become a liberated person; by spiritual realization we become free of all animosity and envy toward other living things.

This higher vision is explained by Śrīla Prabhupāda in the *Transcendental Teachings of Prahlād Mahārāja.* "When a man becomes fully Kṛṣṇa conscious he does not see, 'Here is an animal, here is a cat, here is a dog, and here is a worm.' He sees everything as part and parcel of Kṛṣṇa. This is nicely explained in the *Bhagavad-gītā,* 'One who is actually learned in Kṛṣṇa consciousness becomes a lover of the universe.' Unless one is situated on the Kṛṣṇa conscious platform, there is no question of universal brotherhood."

Brings Real Happiness

Everyone is thirsting for true and lasting happiness. But because material pleasure is limited and temporary, it is compared to a tiny drop of moisture in the desert. It gives us no permanent relief, because material sensations and relationships lack the potency to satisfy the spiritual desires of the soul. But the chanting of Hare Kṛṣṇa provides complete satisfaction because it places us in direct contact with God and His spiritual pleasure potency. God is full of all bliss, and when we enter His association, we can also experience the same transcendental happiness.

In the Vedic literature there is an interesting account of how the pleasure of chanting far exceeds any material benefit. Once a poor *brāhmaṇa* priest worshiped the demigod Lord Śiva for a material benediction. Lord Śiva, however, advised him to go to the sage Sanātana Gosvāmī to obtain his heart's desire. Upon learning that Sanātana Gosvāmī had a mystical stone capable of producing gold, the poor *brāhmaṇa* asked if he could have it. Sanātana consented and told the *brāhmaṇa* he could take the stone from its resting place in his garbage pile. The *brāhmaṇa* departed in great joy, for he could now get as much gold as he desired simply by touching the stone to iron. But afterward he thought, "If a touchstone is the best benediction, why did Sanātana Gosvāmī keep it with the garbage?"

He returned to Sanātana Gosvāmī to satisfy his curiosity. The sage then informed him, "Actually, this is not the best benediction. But are you prepared to take the best benediction from me?"

"Yes," the poor brāhmaṇa replied. "I have come to you for the best benediction." Sanātana Gosvāmī then told him to throw the touchstone in the water nearby and then return. The poor *brāhmaṇa* did so, and when he came back, the saintly Sanātana initiated him into the chanting of the Hare Kṛṣṇa *mantra,* the sublime method for experiencing the highest spiritual pleasure.

Liberation from Karma

The law of *karma* means that for every material action performed, nature forces an equivalent reaction upon the performer, or, as the Bible states, "As ye sow, so shall ye reap."

Material activities can be compared to seeds. Initially they are performed, or planted, and over the course of time they gradually fructify, releasing their resultant reactions. Enmeshed in this web of actions and reactions, we are forced to accept one material body after another to experience our karmic destiny. But freedom from *karma* is possible by sincere chanting of Kṛṣṇa's transcendental names. Since God's names are filled with transcendental energy, when the living being associates with the divine sound vibration, he is freed from the endless cycle of *karma.*

Just as seeds fried in a pan lose their potency to sprout, so karmic reactions are rendered impotent by the power of the holy names of God. Kṛṣṇa is like the sun. The sun is so powerful that it can purify whatever comes into contact with it. If any object enters the sun globe, it is immediately transformed into fire. Similarly, when our consciousness is absorbed in the transcendental sound of Kṛṣṇa, His internal energies act to purify us of all karmic reactions. In his commentary on *Śrīmad-Bhāgavatam*, Śrīla Prabhupāda stresses, "The holy name is so spiritually potent that simply by chanting the holy name one can be freed from the reactions to all sinful activity."

Freedom from Reincarnation

The *Vedas* teach that the living entity, the soul, is eternal, but due to past activities and material desires, it perpetually accepts different material bodies. As long as we have material desires, nature, acting under God's direction, will award us one material body after another. This is called transmigration of the soul, or reincarnation. Actually, this changing of bodies is not surprising, because even in this life we go through many bodies. First we have the body of an infant, then a child, later an adult, and finally the form of an old man or woman. Similarly, after the passing of our old body, we get a new one.

Liberation from this cycle, known as *saṁsāra,* or the endless wheel of birth and death, is possible by freeing our consciousness from material desires. By chanting Hare Kṛṣṇa, we revive the natural spiritual desires of the soul. Just as the nature of the body is to be attracted to sense gratification, the nature of the soul is to be attracted to God. Chanting awakens our original God consciousness and our desire to serve and associate with Him. By this simple change in consciousness, we can transcend the cycle of reincarnation.

Śrīla Prabhupāda discusses this in his commentary on the *Bhagavad-gītā*. "The cumulative effect of the thoughts and actions of one's life influences one's thoughts at death; therefore the actions of this life determine one's future state of being. If one is transcendentally absorbed in Kṛṣṇa's service, then his next body will be transcendental [spiritual], not physical. Therefore the chanting of the Hare Kṛṣṇa *mantra* is the best process for successfully changing one's state of being to transcendental life."

The Ultimate Benefit-Love of God

The final goal and the highest fruit of chanting is complete God realization and pure love of God.

As our consciousness becomes increasingly purified, our steady spiritual advancement is reflected in our character and behavior. As the sun approaches the horizon, it is preceded by increasing warmth and illumination. Similarly, as realization of Kṛṣṇa's holy name is revived within the heart, this increasing spiritual awareness manifests in all aspects of our personality. Ultimately, the eternal, loving relationship between God and the living being is revived. Before entering the material world, each soul had a unique spiritual relationship with God. This loving relationship is thousands of times greater and more intense than any love experienced in the material world. This is described in the *Caitanya-*

caritāmṛta: "Pure love for Kṛṣṇa is eternally established in the heart of living entities. It is not something to be gained from another source. When the heart is purified by hearing and chanting, the living entity is awakened."

In our eternal, constitutional position in the spiritual world, we are able to associate with God directly, serving Him in a spiritual form just suitable for our mood of love and devotion. In this relationship of spiritual love, the pure devotee is absorbed in transcendental ecstasy. This state of ecstasy is described in *The Nectar of Devotion.* "At that time one's heart becomes illuminated like the sun. The sun is far above the planetary systems, and there is no possibility of its being covered by any kind of cloud. Similarly, when a devotee is purified like the sun, from his heart there is a diffusion of ecstatic love more glorious than the sunshine."

Special Boons Obtained by Chanting– Selected Verses from the Scriptures

hare kṛṣṇa hare kṛṣṇa
kṛṣṇa kṛṣṇa hare hare
hare rāma hare rāma
rāma rāma hare hare
iti ṣoḍaśakaṁ nāmnāṁ
kali-kalmaṣa-nāśanaṁ
nātaḥ paratаropāyaḥ
sarva-vedeṣu dṛśyate

(Kali-santaraṇa Upaniṣad)

"Hare Kṛṣṇa, Hare Kṛṣṇa, Kṛṣṇa Kṛṣṇa, Hare Hare/ Hare Rāma, Hare Rāma, Rāma Rāma, Hare Hare—these sixteen names composed of thirty-two syllables are the only means to counteract the evil effects of Kali-yuga.After searching through all the Vedic literature, one cannot find a method of religion more sublime for this age than the chanting of Hare Kṛṣṇa."

nāmno hi yāvatī śaktiḥ
pāpa-nirharaṇe hareḥ
tāvat kartuṁ na śaknoti
pātakaṁ pātakī naraḥ

(Bṛhad-viṣṇu Purāṇa)

"Simply by chanting one holy name of Hari, a sinful man can counteract the reactions to more sins than he is able to commit."

avaśenāpi yan-nāmni
kīrtite sarva-pātakaiḥ
pumān vimucyate sadyaḥ
siṁha-trastair mṛgair iva

(Garuḍa Purāṇa)

"If one chants the holy name of the Lord, even in a helpless condition or without desiring to do so, all the reactions of his sinful life depart, just as when a lion roars, all the small animals flee in fear."

sakṛd uccāritaṁ yena
harir ity akṣara-dvayam
baddha-parikaras tena
mokṣāya gamanaṁ prati

(Skanda Purāṇa)

"By once chanting the holy name of the Lord, which consists of the two syllables ha-ri, one guarantees his path to liberation."

patitaḥ skhalito bhagnaḥ
sandaṣṭas tapta āhataḥ
harir ity avaśenāha
pumān nārhati yātanāḥ

(Śrīmad-Bhāgavatam 6.2.15)

"If one chants the holy name of Hari and then dies because of an accidental misfortune, such as falling from the top of a house, slipping and suffering broken bones while traveling on the road, being bitten by a serpent, being afflicted with pain and high fever, or being injured by a weapon, one is immediately absolved from having to enter hellish life, even though he is sinful."

āpannaḥ saṁsṛtiṁ ghorāṁ
yan-nāma vivaśo gṛṇan
tataḥ sadyo vimucyeta
yad bibheti svayaṁ bhayam

(Śrīmad-Bhāgavatam 1.1.14)

"Living beings who are entangled in the complicated meshes of birth and death can be freed immediately by even unconsciously chanting the holy name of Kṛṣṇa, which is feared by fear personified."

PURPORT

Vāsudeva, or Lord Kṛṣṇa, the Absolute Personality of Godhead, is the supreme controller of everything. There is no one in creation who is not afraid of the rage of the Almighty. Great asuras like Rāvaṇa, Hiraṇyakaśipu, Kaṁsa, and others who were very powerful living entities were all killed by the Personality of Godhead. And the almighty Vāsudeva has empowered His name with the powers of His personal Self. Everything is related to Him, and everything has its identity in Him. It is stated herein that the name of Kṛṣṇa is feared even by fear personified. This indicates that the name of Kṛṣṇa is nondifferent from Kṛṣṇa. Therefore, the name of Kṛṣṇa is as powerful as Lord Kṛṣṇa Himself. There is no difference at all. Anyone, therefore, can take advantage of the holy names of Lord Śrī Kṛṣṇa even in the midst of greatest dangers. The transcendental name of Kṛṣṇa, even though uttered unconsciously or by force of circumstances, can help one obtain freedom from the hurdle of birth and death.

nātaḥ paraṁ karma-nibandha-kṛntanaṁ
mumukṣatāṁ tīrtha-padānukīrtanāt
na yat punaḥ karmasu sajjate mano
rajas-tamobhyāṁ kalilaṁ tato 'nyathā

(Śrīmad-Bhāgavatam 6.2.46)

"Therefore one who desires freedom from material bondage should adopt the process of chanting and glorifying the name, fame, form and pastimes of the Supreme Personality of Godhead, at whose feet all the holy places stand. One cannot derive the proper benefit from other methods, such as pious atonement, speculative knowledge and meditation in mystic yoga, because even after following such methods one takes to fruitive activities again, unable to control his mind, which is contaminated by the base qualities of nature, namely passion and ignorance."

mantratas tantrataś chidraṁ
deśa-kālārha-vastutaḥ
sarvaṁ karoti niśchidram
anusaṅkīrtanaṁ tava

(Śrīmad-Bhāgavatam 8.23.16)

"There may be discrepancies in pronouncing the mantras and observing the regulative principles, and, moreover, there may be discrepancies in regard to time, place, person and paraphernalia. But when Your Lordship's holy name is chanted, everything becomes faultless."

sāṅketyaṁ pārihāsyaṁ vā
stobhaṁ helanam eva vā
vaikuṇṭha-nāma-grahaṇam
aśeṣāgha-haraṁ viduḥ

(Śrīmad-Bhāgavatam 6.2.14)

"One who chants the holy name of the Lord is immediately freed from the reactions of unlimited sins, even if he chants indirectly [to indicate something else], jokingly, for musical entertainment, or even neglectfully. This is accepted by all the learned scholars of the scriptures."

yathāgadaṁ vīryatamam
upayuktaṁ yadṛcchayā
ajānato 'py ātma-guṇaṁ
kuryān mantro 'py udāhṛtaḥ

(Śrīmad-Bhāgavatam 6.2.19)

"If a person unaware of the effective potency of a certain medicine takes that medicine or is forced to take it, it will act even without his knowledge because its potency does not depend on the patient's understanding. Similarly, even though one does not know the value of chanting the holy name of the Lord, if one chants knowingly or unknowingly, the chanting will be very effective."

saṅkīrtyamāno bhagavān anantaḥ
śrutānubhāvo vyasanaṁ hi puṁsām

praviśya cittaṁ vidhunoty aśeṣaṁ
yathā tamo 'rko 'bhram ivāti-vātaḥ
(Śrīmad-Bhāgavatam 12.12.48)

"When people properly glorify the Supreme Personality of Godhead or simply hear about His power, the Lord personally enters their hearts and cleanses away every trace of misfortune, just as the sun removes the darkness or as a powerful wind drives away the clouds."

yan-nāmadheyaṁ mriyamāṇa āturaḥ
patan skhalan vā vivaśo gṛṇan pumān
vimukta-karmārgala uttamāṁ gatiṁ
prāpnoti yakṣyanti na taṁ kalau janāḥ
(Śrīmad-Bhāgavatam 12.3.44)

"Terrified, about to die, a man collapses on his bed. Although his voice is faltering and he is hardly conscious of what he is saying, if he utters the holy name of the Supreme Lord he can be freed from the reaction of his fruitive work and achieve the supreme destination. But still people in the age of Kali will not worship the Supreme Lord."

etan nirvidyamānānām
icchatām akuto-bhayam
yogināṁ nṛpa nirṇītaṁ
harer nāmānukīrtanam
(Śrīmad-Bhāgavatam 2.1.11)

"O King, constant chanting of the holy name of the Lord after the ways of the great authorities is the doubtless and fearless way of success for all, including those who are free from all material desires, those who are desirous of all material enjoyment, and also those who are self-satisfied by dint of transcendental knowledge."

stenaḥ surā-po mitra-dhrug
brahma-hā guru-talpa-gaḥ
strī-rāja-pitṛ-go-hantā
ye ca pātakino 'pare
sarveṣām apy aghavatām
idam eva suniṣkṛtam
nāma-vyāharaṇaṁ viṣṇor
yatas tad-viṣayā matiḥ

(Śrīmad-Bhāgavatam 6.2.9-10)

"The chanting of the holy name of Lord Viṣṇu is the best process of atonement for a thief of gold or other valuables, for a drunkard, for one who betrays a friend or relative, for one who kills a brāhmaṇa, or for one who indulges in sex with the wife of his guru or another superior. It is also the best method of atonement for one who murders women, the king or his father, for one who slaughters cows, and for all other sinful men. Simply by chanting the holy name of Lord Viṣṇu, such sinful persons may attract the attention of the Supreme Lord, who therefore considers, 'Because this man has chanted My holy name, My duty is to give him protection.'"

tasmāt saṅkīrtanaṁ viṣṇor
jagan-maṅgalam aṁhasām
mahatām api kauravya
viddhy aikāntika-niṣkṛtam

(Śrīmad-Bhāgavatam 6.3.31)

"Śukadeva Gosvāmī continued: My dear King, the chanting of the holy name of the Lord is able to uproot even the reactions of the greatest sins. Therefore the chanting of the saṅkīrtana movement is the most auspicious activity in the entire universe. Please try to understand this so that others will take it seriously."

The Deliverance of Ajamila

The first chapter of the sixth canto of *Śrīmad-Bhāgavatam* relates the history of Ajāmila, who was considered a greatly sinful man, but was liberated when four order carriers of Viṣṇu came to rescue him from the hands of the order carriers of *Yamarāja*. To prove the strength of devotional service, Śukadeva Gosvāmī described the history of Ajāmila. Ajāmila was a resident of Kānyakubja (the modern Kanauj). He was trained by his parents to become a perfect *brāhmaṇa* by studying the Vedas and following the regulative principles, but because of his past, this youthful *brāhmaṇa* was somehow attracted by a prostitute, and because of her association he became most fallen and abandoned all regulative principles. Ajāmila begot in the womb of the prostitute ten sons, the last of whom was called Nārāyaṇa. At the time of Ajāmila's death, when the order carriers of *Yamarāja* came to take him, he loudly called the name Nārāyaṇa in fear because he was attached to his youngest son. Thus he remembered the original Nārāyaṇa, Lord Viṣṇu. Although he did not chant the holy name of Nārāyaṇa completely offenselessly, it acted nevertheless. As soon as he chanted the holy name of Nārāyaṇa, the order carriers of Lord Viṣṇu immediately appeared on the scene. A discussion ensued between the order carriers of Lord Viṣṇu and those of *Yamarāja*. .

The *Viṣṇudūtas* said, "Now impious acts are being performed even in an assembly of devotees, for a person who is not punishable is going to be punished in the assembly of *Yamarāja*. The mass of people are helpless and must depend upon the government for their safety and security, but if the government takes advantage of this to harm the citizens, where will they go? We see perfectly that Ajāmila should not be punished, although you are attempting to take him to *Yamarāja* for punishment."

It was due to Ajāmila's glorifying the holy name of the Supreme Lord that he was not punishable. The Viṣṇudūtas explained this as follows: "Simply by once chanting the holy name of Nārāyaṇa, this *brāhmaṇa* has become free from the reactions of sinful life. Indeed, he has been freed not only from the sins of this life, but from the sins of many, many thousands of other lives. He has already undergone true atonement for all his sinful actions. If one atones according to the directions of the *śāstras*, one does not actually become free from sinful reactions, but if one chants the holy name of the Lord, even a glimpse of such chanting can immediately free one from all sins. Chanting the glories of the Lord's holy name awakens all good fortune. Therefore there is no doubt that Ajāmila, being completely free from all sinful reactions, should not be punished by *Yamarāja*."

As they were saying this, the *Viṣṇudūtas* released Ajāmila from the ropes of the *Yamadūtas* and left for their own abode. The *brāhmaṇa* Ajāmila, however, offered his respectful obeisances to the *Viṣṇudūtas*. He could understand how fortunate he was to have chanted the holy name of Nārāyaṇa at the end of his life. Indeed, he could realize the full significance of this good fortune. Having thoroughly understood the discussion between the *Yamadūtas* and the *Viṣṇudūtas*, he became a pure devotee of the Supreme Personality of Godhead. He lamented very much for how very sinful he had been, and he condemned himself again and again.

Finally, because of his association with the *Viṣṇudūtas*, Ajāmila, his original consciousness aroused, gave up everything and went to Hardwar, where he engaged in devotional service without deviation, always thinking of the Supreme Personality of Godhead. Thus the *Viṣṇudūtas* went there, seated him on a golden throne and took him away to *Vaikuṇṭhaloka*.

In summary, although the sinful Ajāmila meant to call his son, the holy name of Lord Nārāyaṇa, even though chanted in the preliminary stage, *nāmābhāsa*, was able to give him liberation. Therefore one who chants the holy name of the Lord with faith and devotion is certainly exalted. He is protected even in his material, conditional life.

About The Author

His Divine Grace A.C. Bhaktivedanta Swami Prabhupāda appeared in this world in 1896 in Calcutta, India. He first met his spiritual master, Śrīla Bhaktisiddhānta Sarasvatī Gosvāmi, in Calcutta in 1922. Bhaktisiddhānta Sarasvatī, a prominent religious scholar and the founder of sixty-four Gauḍīya Maṭhas (Vedic institutes) in India, liked this educated young man and convinced him to dedicate his life to teaching Vedic knowledge. Śrīla Prabhupāda became his student and, in 1933, his formally initiated disciple.

At their first meeting Śrīla Bhaktisiddhānta Sarasvatī requested Śrīla Prabhupāda to broadcast Vedic knowledge in English. In the years that followed, Śrīla Prabhupāda wrote a commentary on the Bhagavad-gītā, assisted the Gauḍīya Maṭha in its work, and, in 1944, started Back to Godhead, an English fortnightly magazine. Single-handedly, Śrīla Prabhupāda edited it, typed the manuscripts, checked the proofs, and even distributed the individual copies. The magazine is now being continued by his disciples.

In 1950 Śrīla Prabhupāda retired from married life, adopting the vānaprastha (retired) order to devote more time to his studies and writing. He traveled to the holy city of Vṛndāvana, where he lived in humble circumstances in the historic temple of Rādhā-Dāmodara. There he engaged for several years in deep study and writing. He accepted the renounced order of life (sannyāsa) in 1959. At Rādhā-Dāmodara, Śrīla Prabhupāda began work on his life's masterpiece: a multivolume commentated translation of the eighteen-thousand-verse Śrīmad-Bhāgavatam (Bhāgavata Purāṇa). He also wrote Easy Journey to Other Planets.

After publishing three volumes of the Bhāgavatam, Śrīla Prabhupāda came to the United States, in September 1965, to fulfill the mission of his spiritual master. Subsequently, His Divine Grace wrote more than fifty volumes of authoritative commentated translations and summary studies of the philosophical and religious classics of India.

When he first arrived by freighter in New York City, Śrīla Prabhupāda was practically penniless. Only after almost a year of great difficulty did he establish the International Society for Krishna Consciousness, in July of 1966. Before he passed away on November 14, 1977, he had guided the Society and seen it grow to a worldwide confederation of more than one hundred āśramas, schools, temples, institutes, and farm communities.

In 1972 His Divine Grace introduced the Vedic system of primary and secondary education in the West by founding the gurukula school in Dallas, Texas. Since then his disciples have established similar schools throughout the United States and the rest of the world.

Śrīla Prabhupāda also inspired the construction of several large international cultural centers in India. The center at Śrīdhāma Māyāpur is the site for a planned spiritual city, an ambitious project for which construction will extend over many years to come. In Vṛndāvana are the magnificent Kṛṣṇa-Balarāma Temple and International Guesthouse, gurukula school, and Śrīla Prabhupāda Memorial and Museum. There are also major cultural and educational centers in Bombay, Delhi and Ahmedabad. Major centers are planned in a dozen other important locations on the Indian subcontinent.

Śrīla Prabhupāda's most significant contribution, however, is his books. Highly respected by scholars for their authority, depth, and clarity, they are used as textbooks in numerous college courses. His writings have been translated into over fifty languages. The Bhaktivedanta Book Trust, established in 1972 to publish the works of His Divine Grace, has thus become the world's largest publisher of books in the field of Indian religion and philosophy.

In just twelve years, despite his advanced age, Śrīla Prabhupāda circled the globe fourteen times on lecture tours that took him to six continents. Yet this vigorous schedule did not slow his prolific literary output. His writings constitute a veritable library of Vedic philosophy, religion, literature, and culture.

Glossary

A

Ācārya—a spiritual master who teaches by his own example, and who sets the proper religious example for all human beings.

Āśrama—a spiritual order of life in the Vedic *varṇāśrama* system. The four *āśramas* are *brahmacārī* or student life, *gṛhastha* or married life, *vānaprastha* or retired life, and *sannyāsa* or the renounced order of life; the home of the spiritual master, a place where spiritual practices are executed.

Ārati—a ceremony in which one greets and worships the Lord in His form of a Deity by offerings such as incense, a flame, water, a fine cloth, a fragrant flower, a peacock-feather, and yak-tail whisk, accompanied by ringing of a bell and chanting of *mantras*.

Asat—not eternal, temporary.

Avatāra—literally "one who descends." A partially or fully empowered incarnation of Lord Kṛṣṇa who descends from the spiritual sky to the material universe with a particular mission described in the scriptures. Lord Śrī Kṛṣṇa is the original Personality of Godhead from whom all *avatāras* originate. There are two broad categories of *avatāras*. Some, like Śrī Kṛṣṇa, Śrī Rāma and Śrī Nṛsiṁha, are Viṣṇu-tattva, i.e. direct forms of God Himself, the source of all power. Others are ordinary souls (*jīvatattva*) who are called *śaktyāveśa avatāras*, and are empowered by the Lord to execute a certain purpose.

B

Bhagavad-gītā—a seven-hundred verse record of a conversation between Lord Kṛṣṇa and His disciple, Arjuna, from the *Bhīṣma Parva* of the *Mahābhārata* of Vedavyāsa. The conversation took place between two armies minutes before the start of an immense fratricidal battle. Kṛṣṇa teaches the science of the Absolute Truth and the importance of devotional service to the despondent Arjuna, and it contains the essence of all Vedic wisdom. Śrīla Prabhupāda's annotated English translation is called *Bhagavad-gītā As It Is*; This most essential text of spiritual knowledge, The Song of the Lord, contains Kṛṣṇa's instructions to Arjuna at Kurukṣetra. It is found in the *Mahābhārata*. The *Mahābhārata* is classified as *smṛti-śāstra*, a supplement of the *śruti-śāstra*. *Śruti*, the core Vedic literature, includes the four Vedas (*Ṛg*, *Sāma*, *Yajur* and *Atharva*) and the *Upaniṣads*. *Śruti* advances the understanding of the absolute. B*hagavad-gītā* is also known as *Gītopaniṣad*, or a *śruti* text spoken by the Supreme Personality of Godhead Himself. Therefore, Śrīla Prabhupāda wrote in a letter, the

Gītā should be taken as *śruti*. But they take it as smṛti because it is part of the *smṛti* (*Mahābhārata*). In one sense it is both *śruti* and *smṛti*. In only 700 verses, the *Bhagavadgītā* summarizes all Vedic knowledge about the soul, God, *sanātana-dharma*, sacrifice, *yoga*, *karma*, reincarnation, the modes of material nature, *Vedānta* and pure devotion.

Bhāgavata—anything related to Bhagavān, the Supreme Lord, especially the devotee of the Lord and the scripture *Śrīmad-Bhāgavatam*.

Bhakta—a devotee of the Lord; one who performs devotional service (*bhakti*).

Bhakti—devotional service to the Supreme Lord; purified service of the senses of the Lord by one's own senses; love and devotion to the Supreme Personality of Godhead, Lord Kṛṣṇa. The formal systematization of devotion is called *bhakti-yoga*.

Bhakti-yoga—the system of cultivation of pure devotional service to the Supreme Personality of Godhead, Lord Kṛṣṇa, which is not tinged by sense gratification or philosophical speculation. It consists of nine *aṅgas* or parts: (1) *śravaṇaṁ*–hearing about the transcendental holy name, form, and other qualities of the Lord (2) *kīrtanaṁ*– chanting about these qualities, (3) *viṣṇoḥ smaraṇaṁ*–remembering them, (4) *pāda-sevanam*–serving the lotus feet of the Lord, (5) *arcanaṁ*–worshipping the Deity of the Lord, (6) *vandanaṁ*–offering prayers to the Lord, (7) *dāsyaṁ* – serving His mission, (8) *sakhyam*–making friends with the Lord, and (9) *ātma-nivedanam*–surrendering everything unto Him.

Brahmā—the first created being of the universe; directed by Lord Viṣṇu, he creates all life forms in the universe and rules the mode of passion.

Brahmacārī—celibate student, living in the first order of Vedic spiritual Life and practicing the vow of strict abstinence from sex indulgence.

Brāhmaṇa—a member of the intellectual, priestly class; a person wise in Vedic knowledge, fixed in goodness and knowledge of Brahman, the Absolute Truth; one of the four orders of Vedic society. Their occupation consists of learning and teaching Vedic literature, learning and teaching Deity worship, and receiving and giving charity.

Brahmajyoti—the impersonal bodily effulgence emanating from the transcendental body of the Supreme Lord Kṛṣṇa, which constitutes the brilliant illumination of the spiritual sky; From Kṛṣṇa's transcendental personal form of eternity, knowledge and bliss emanates a shining effulgence called the *brahmajyoti* (light of Brahman). The material *prakṛti*, the souls or *jīvas* who desire to enjoy matter, and *kāla* (time), are situated within this *brahmajyoti*, which is pure existence devoid of difference and activity. It is the impersonal Brahman of the Māyāvādīs, and the Clear Light of some Buddhist sects. For many mystics and philosophers the world over, the *brahmajyoti* is the indefinable One from which all things emerge in the beginning and merge into at the end. The *brahmajyoti* is Kṛṣṇa's feature of sat (eternality) separated from *cit* (knowledge) and *ānanda* (bliss).

Brahmaloka—the abode of Lord Brahmā, the highest planet in this world.

Brahman—(1) the infinitesimal spiritual individual soul, (2) the impersonal, all-pervasive aspect of the Supreme, (3) the Supreme Personality of Godhead and (4) the *mahat-tattva*, or total material substance

Buddhi-yoga—another term for *bhakti-yoga* (devotional service to Kṛṣṇa), indicating that it represents the highest use of intelligence (*buddhi*).

D

Dharma—religious principles; one's natural occupation; the quality of rendering service, which is the essential, eternal quality of the soul, regarded as inseparable from it. The Sanskrit term *dharma* is variously translated as duty, virtue, morality, righteousness, or religion, but no single English word conveys the actual import of *dharma*. Dharma ultimately means to surrender to the

Supreme Lord, as Lord Kṛṣṇa commands Arjuna in the *Gītā*.

Dvāpara-yuga—the third age of the cycle of a *mahā-yuga*. It lastsmore than 864,000 years.

G

Gṛhastha—regulated householder life. One who leads a God conscious married life and raises a family in Kṛṣṇa consciousness according to the Vedic social system; the second order of Vedic spiritual life.

Gosvāmī—a *svāmī*, one who is fully able to control his senses.

Guru—spiritual master; one of the three spiritual authorities for a Vaiṣṇava. Literally, this term means heavy. The spiritual master is heavy with knowledge.

H

Hari-kīrtana—congregational chanting of the holy names of the Supreme Lord, the recommended sacrifice for this age.

J

Jñāna—knowledge. Material *jñāna* does not go beyond the material body and its expansions. Transcendental *jñāna* discriminates between matter and spirit. Perfect *jñāna* is knowledge of the body, the soul and the Supreme Lord.

Jñāna-yoga—the process of approaching the Supreme by the cultivation of knowledge; the predominantly empirical process of linking with the Supreme, which is executed when one is still attached to mental speculation.

Jñānī—one who is engaged in the cultivation of knowledge, especially by philosophical speculation. Upon attaining perfection, a *jñānī* surrenders to Kṛṣṇa.

K

Kali-yuga—the present age, the Age of Kalī, the Age of Quarrel and Hypocrisy. The fourth and last age in the cycle of a *mahā-yuga*. It began 5,000 years ago, and lasts for a total of 432,000 years. It is characterized by irreligious practice and stringent material miseries. The most recommended process of spiritual upliftment in this age is saṅkīrtana, the congregational glorification of the Lord through chanting His holy name.

Karma—1. material action performed according to scriptural regulations; 2. action pertaining to the development of the material body; 3. any material action which will incur a subsequent reaction; 4. the material reaction one incurs due to fruitive activities; This Sanskrit word means 'action' or, more specifically, any material action that brings a reaction binding us to the material world. According to the law of karma, if we cause pain and suffering to other living beings, we must endure pain and suffering in return; One of the five tattvas, or Vedic ontological truths: the activity or work which the embodied living entity performs with the karmendriya, as well as the resultant reaction. The soul receives the due reaction to work by taking his next birth in a subhuman species, or the human species, or a superhuman species. Or the soul may be liberated from birth and death altogether. All this depends upon whether the karma performed within this lifetime is ignorant, passionate, good or transcendental. Karma dedicated in sacrifice as directed by Vedic injunctions raises the quality of a human being's work. Sacrifice culminates in activity dedicated only to Lord Kṛṣṇa's service. Such transcendental karma is called naiṣkarma.

Karma-yoga—action in devotional service; the path of God realization through dedicating the fruits of one's work to God.

Karmī—a fruitive laborer, one who is attached to the fruits of work, a materialist who works hard to enjoy material life.

Kṣatriya—second of the four social orders of the *varṇāśrama* system; a warrior who is inclined to fight and lead others; the administrative or protective occupation.

L

Līlā—a transcendental "pastime," or activity, performed by the Supreme Lord.

Loka—a planet.

M

Mahā-mantra—a sixteen-word prayer composed of the names Hare, Kṛṣṇa, and Rāma: Hare Kṛṣṇa, Hare Kṛṣṇa, Kṛṣṇa Kṛṣṇa,

Hare Hare, Hare Rāma, Hare Rāma, Rāma Rāma, Hare Hare.

Hare is an address to *Harā,* another name for His eternal consort, Śrīmatī Rādhārāṇī. Kṛṣṇa, "the all-attractive one," and Rāma, "the all-pleasing one," are names of God. The chanting of this *mantra* is the most recommended means for spiritual progress in this age of Kali, as it cleanses the mind of all impurities, and helps to understand one's true identity as an eternal spiritual being. Lord Caitanya personally designated it as the *mahā-mantra* and practically demonstrated the effects of the chanting.

Mahātma—a "great soul"; a liberated person who is fully Kṛṣṇa conscious.

Mantra—a transcendental sound or Vedic hymn, a prayer or chant; a pure sound vibration when repeated over and over delivers the mind from its material inclinations and illusion. The Vedic scriptures are composed of many thousands of *mantras.*

Māyā—Māyāvāda philosophy. Māyāvāda in Sanskrit means doctrine of illusion. In India, the philosophies of the Buddha and of Śaṅkarācārya are called Māyāvāda. The second grew out of the first. The fundamental principles accepted by both are the following: 1) name, form, individuality, thoughts, desires and words arise from māyā or illusion, not God; 2) māyā cannot be rationally explained, since the very idea that anything needs explaining is itself māyā; 3) the individual self or soul is not eternal, because upon liberation it ceases to exist; 4) like māyā, the state of liberation is beyond all explanation. The main difference between the two is that Śaṅkarācārya's Māyāvāda asserts that beyond māyā is an eternal impersonal monistic reality, Brahman, the nature of which is the self. Buddhism, however, aims at extinction (nirodha) as the final goal. Of the two, Śaṅkarācārya's Māyāvāda is more dangerous, as it apparently derives its authority from the Vedas. Much word-jugglery is employed to defend the Vedic origins of Śaṅkarācārya's Māyāvāda. But ultimately Māyāvādīs dispense with Vedic authority by concluding that the Supreme cannot be known through śabda, that the name of Kṛṣṇa is a material vibration, that the form of Kṛṣṇa is illusion, and so on. The Śaṅkarites agree with the Buddhists that nāma-rūpa (name and form) must always be māyā. Therefore Vaiṣṇavas reject both kinds of Māyāvāda as atheism. Buddhists generally do not deny that they are atheists, whereas the Śaṅkarite Māyāvādīs claim to be theists. But actually they are monists and pantheists. Their claim to theism is refuted by their belief that the Supreme Self is overcome by māyā and becomes the bound soul. Śaṅkarācārya's Māyāvāda is similar in significant ways to the Western doctrine of solipsism. Like solipsism, it arrives at a philosophical dead end. The questions that remain unanswered are: If my consciousness is the only reality, why can't I change the universe at will, simply by thought? And if my own self is the only reality, why am I dependent for my life, learning and happiness upon a world full of living entities that refuse to acknowledge this reality?

Māyā—illusion; an energy of Kṛṣna's which deludes the living entity into forgetfulness of the Supreme Lord. That which is not, unreality, deception, forgetfulness, material illusion. Under illusion a man thinks he can be happy in this temporary material world. The nature of the material world is that the more a man tries to exploit the material situation, the more he is bound by māyā's complexities; This is a Sanskrit term of many meanings. It may mean energy; yoga-māyā is the spiritual energy sustaining the transcendental manifestation of the spiritual Vaikuṇṭha world, while the reflection, mahā-māyā, is the energy of the material world. The Lord's twofold māyā bewilders the jīva, hence māyā also means bewilderment or illusion. Transcendental bewilderment is in love, by which the devotee sees God as his master, friend, dependent or amorous beloved. The material bewilderment of the living entity begins with his attraction to the glare of the brahmajyoti. That attraction leads to his entanglement in the modes of material nature. According to Bhaktisiddhānta Sarasvatī Ṭhākura, māyā also means that which can be measured. This is the feature of Lord Kṛṣṇa's prakṛti that captures the minds of scientific materialists. The Vaiṣṇava and Māyāvāda explanations of māyā are not the same.

Mukti—liberation from material existence.

N

Nivṛtti-mārga—the path of renunciation, which leads to liberation; directions for giving up the material world for higher spiritual understanding.

P

Pravṛtti-mārga—the path of sense enjoyment in accordance with Vedic regulations.

Purāṇas—the eighteen historical supplements to the *vedās*.

S

Śāstra—revealed scripture; Vedic literature.

Sac-cid-ānanda—eternal, blissful and full of knowledge.

Saṅkīrtana—congregational or public glorification of the Supreme Lord Kṛṣṇa through chanting of His holy names, and glorification of His fame and pastimes.

Sāṅkhya—analytical discrimination between spirit and matter and the path of devotional service as described by Lord Kapila, the son of Devahūti.

Sampradāya—a disciplic succession of spiritual masters, along with the followers in that tradition, through which spiritual knowledge is transmitted; school of thought.

Sannyāsī—a person in the renounced order.

Sat—eternal, unlimited existence.

Satya-yuga—the first and best of the four cyclic ages of a *mahā-yuga* in the progression of universal time, lasting 1,728,000 solar years. It is known as the golden age, characterized by virtue, wisdom and religion, when people lived as long as one hundred thousand years.

Śrīmad-Bhāgavatam—the *Purāṇa*, or history, written by Vyāsadeva specifically to give a deep understanding of Lord Śrī Kṛṣṇa.

Śūdras—a member of the fourth social order, laborer class, in the traditional Vedic social system.

T

Tapasya—the voluntary acceptance of hardships for spiritual realization, such as rising early in the morning and taking a bath, fasting on certain days of the month etc.

Tilaka—sacred clay markings placed on the forehead and other parts of the body which designate one as a follower of Viṣṇu, Rāma, Śiva etc.

Tretā-yuga—the second in the cycle of the four ages of the universe or *mahā-yuga*. It lasts 1,296,000 years. Lord Rāmacandra appeared in this age.

U

Upaniṣads—108 philosophical treatises that appear within the *Vedas*.

V

Vaiśya—member of the mercantile or agricultural class, according to the system of four social orders and four spiritual orders.

Vaikuṇṭha—the eternal planets of the spiritual world, the abode of Lord Nārāyaṇa, which lies beyond the coverings of the material universe. Literally, "the place with no anxiety."

Vānaprastha—A retired householder, a member of the third Vedic spiritual order or *āśrama*, who quits home to cultivate renunciation and travels to holy places, in preparation for the renounced order of life.

Varṇāśrama—the system of four social and four spiritual orders of Vedic society, based on the individual's psycho-physical qualities and tendencies toward particular types of work.

Vedānta-sūtra—also known as *Brahma-sūtra*, it is Śrīla Vyāsadeva's conclusive summary of Vedic philosophical knowledge, written in brief codes. All apparent contradictory statements of the vast literature of the *Vedas* are resolved in this work. There are four divisions: (1) reconciliation of all scriptures (2) the consistent reconciliation of apparently conflicting hymns (3) the means or process of attaining the goal (spiritual realization) and (4) the object (or desired fruit) achieved by the spiritual process. The codes of the *Vedānta-sūtra* are very terse, and without a fuller explanation or commentary, their meaning is difficult to grasp. In India all the five main schools of *Vedānta* have explained the *sūtras* through their respective *bhāṣyas* (commentaries). The natural commentary on the *Vedānta-sūtra* is the *Śrīmad-Bhāgavatam.*

Vedas—the original Veda was divided into four by Śrīla Vyāsadeva. The four original Vedic scriptures, *Saṁhitās* (*Ṛg, Sāma, Atharva* and *Yajur*) and the 108 *Upaniṣads*, *Mahābhārata*, *Vedānta-sūtra*, etc. The system of eternal wisdom compiled by Śrīla Vyāsadeva, the literary incarnation of the Supreme Lord, for the gradual upliftment of all mankind from the state of bondage to the state of liberation. The word veda literally means "knowledge", and thus in a wider sense it refers to the whole body of Indian Sanskrit religious literature that is in harmony with the philosophical conclusions found in the original four Vedic *Saṁhitās* and *Upaniṣads.*

Viṣṇudūtas—the messengers of Lord Viṣṇu who come to take perfected devotees back to the spiritual world at the time of death, the personal servants of Lord Viṣṇu, they closely resemble Him in appearance.

Y

Yajña—a Vedic sacrifice; also a name for the Supreme Lord meaning "the personification of sacrifice"; the goal and enjoyer of all sacrifices.

Yamarāja—the demigod who punishes the sinful after death.

Yoga—spiritual discipline to link oneself with the Supreme Lord.

Yogī—a transcendentalist who practices one of the many authorized forms of *yoga* or processes of spiritual purification; one who practices the eight-fold mystic *yoga* process to gain mystic *siddhis* (powers), or to achieve *Paramātmā* realization.

Yuga—an "age." There are four yugas, which cycle perpetually: *Satya-yuga, Tretā-yuga, Dvāpara-yuga* and Kali-Yuga. As the ages proceed from Satyā to Kali, religion and the good qualities of men gradually decline.